You can draw anywhere you want in this book.

Sometimes, the book will point you to places to draw.

Once you start drawing, you will want to draw more.

For example, here is a white circle.  You can make it an apple.

... or a tangerine.  It can become a face too.

... or perhaps a sunny-side up egg.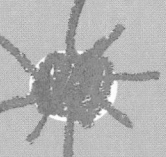

You could turn it into the sun... 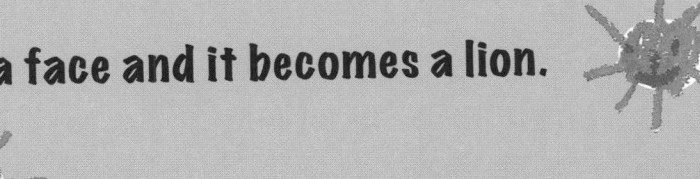 draw a face and it becomes a lion.

Add a body and it looks more like a lion.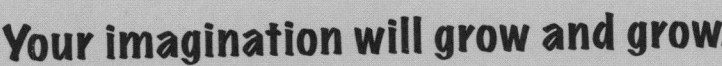

Your imagination will grow and grow.

The more you draw, the better at it you'll become.

The more you use your imagination, the more it grows!

It's OK to draw anything

The suggestions on what and where to draw are only a start.
You will come up with many ideas as you color and draw.
Put those ideas on the page!

It's OK to use anything to draw

Crayons, colored pencils, paint or markers are all great.

It's OK to color in any way you want

Scribble, color neatly, color with dots...
Color and draw however you want.
It's OK to go over the lines.
There are no rules!

It's OK to start anywhere

Start from any page you choose.
You can even draw again where you've drawn already.

Show everyone when you are done

It's done when you think it's done.
What you have created is the only book like it in the whole world.

For example...

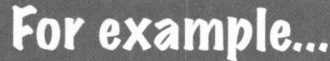

You can use crayons or markers, but it will give it a different look if you paste paper cutouts.

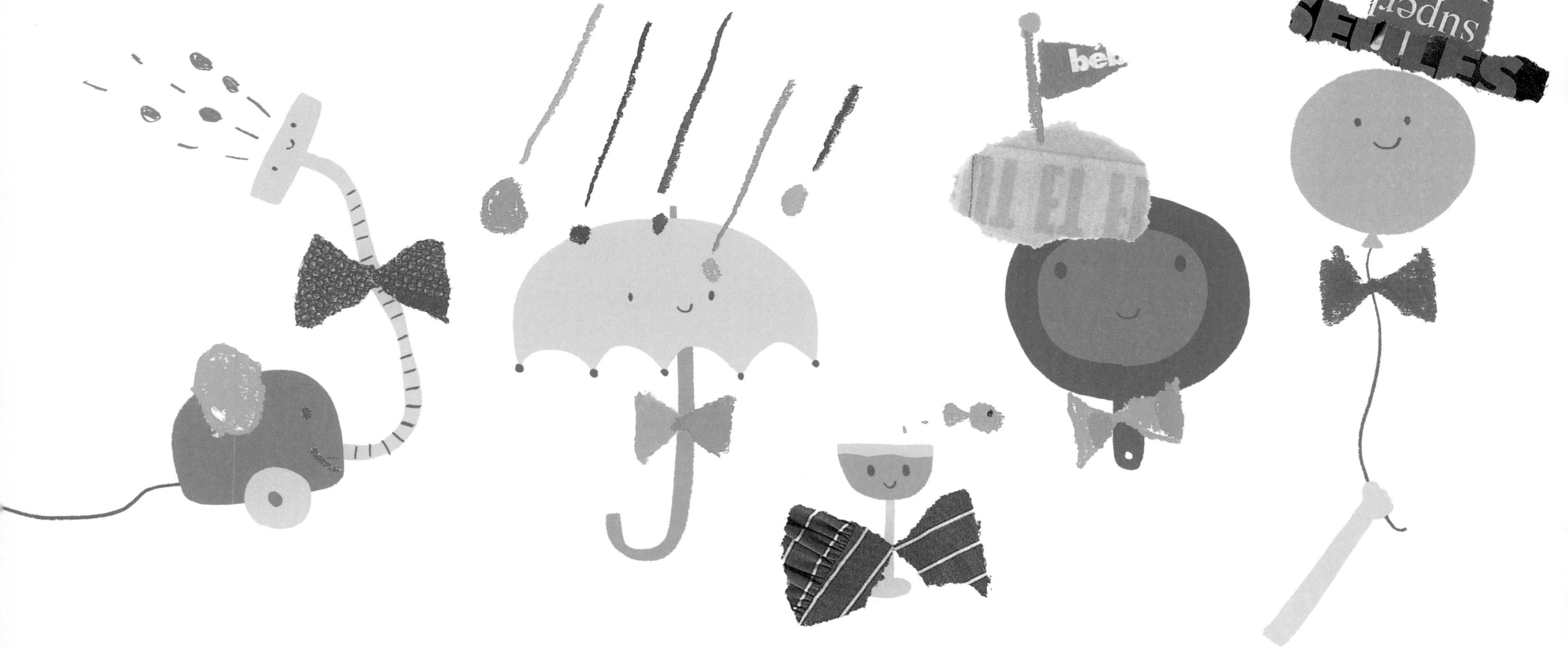

This house is all alone. How can you change that?

This house is all alone. How can you change that?

This house is all alone. How can you change that?

This house is all alone. How can you change that?

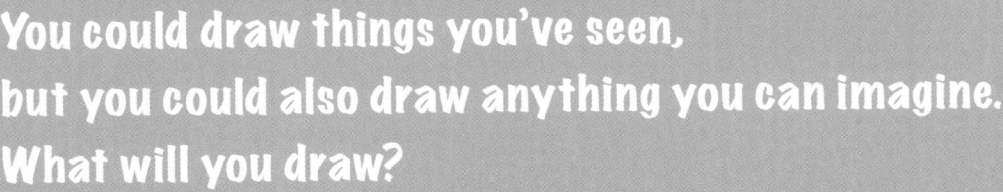

This house is all alone. How can you change that?

You could draw things you've seen,
but you could also draw anything you can imagine.
What will you draw?

For example...

You can draw without staying inside the lines.
Don't think you have to color neatly.

Is there anyone home in these buildings?

What are these wacky ghosts doing?

What colors should the fireworks be?

Since no people are exactly the same, no drawings will be exactly the same.

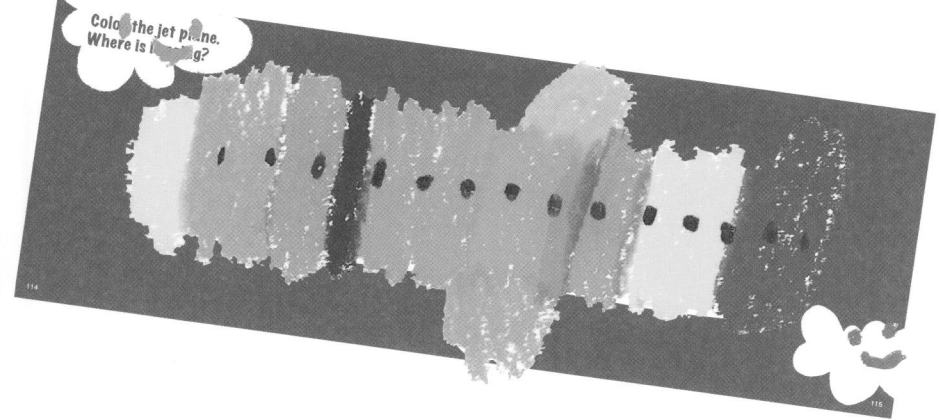

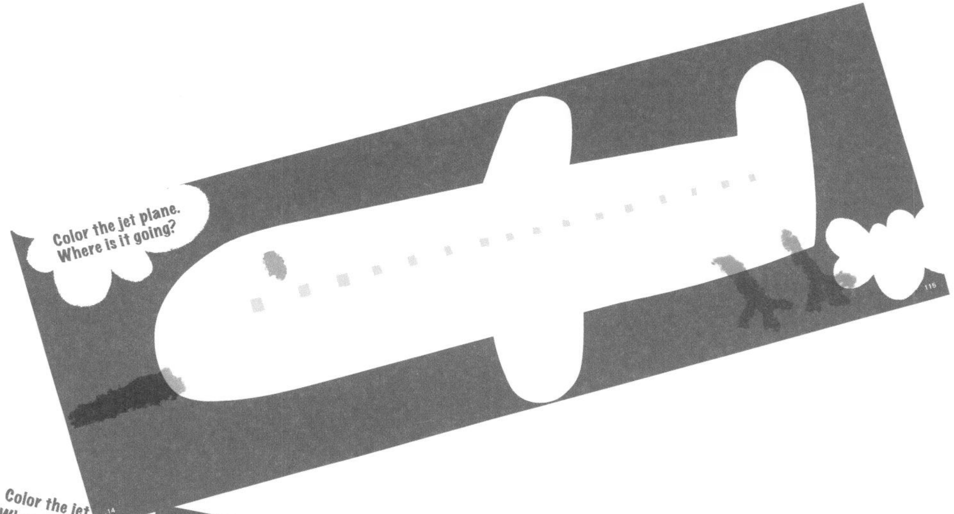

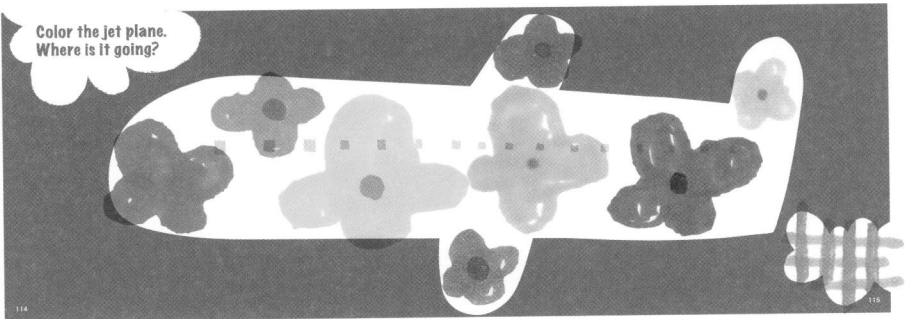

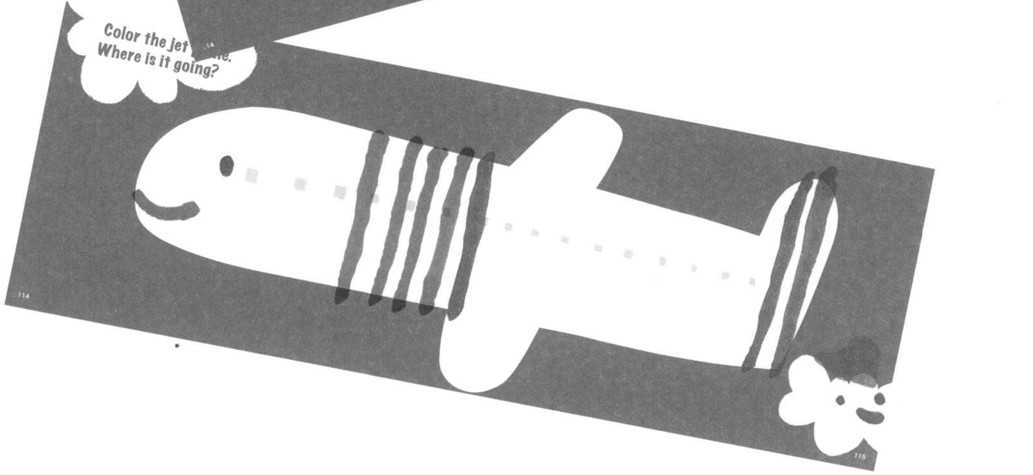

Color the jet plane.
Where is it going?

Color the jet plane.
Where is it going?

Color the jet plane.
Where is it going?

Color the jet plane.
Where is it going?

Draw yourself.

Me

This is your own unique book.

Your
name

Your
age

It's a ladybug fashion show.

What are they wearing? Draw what you think!

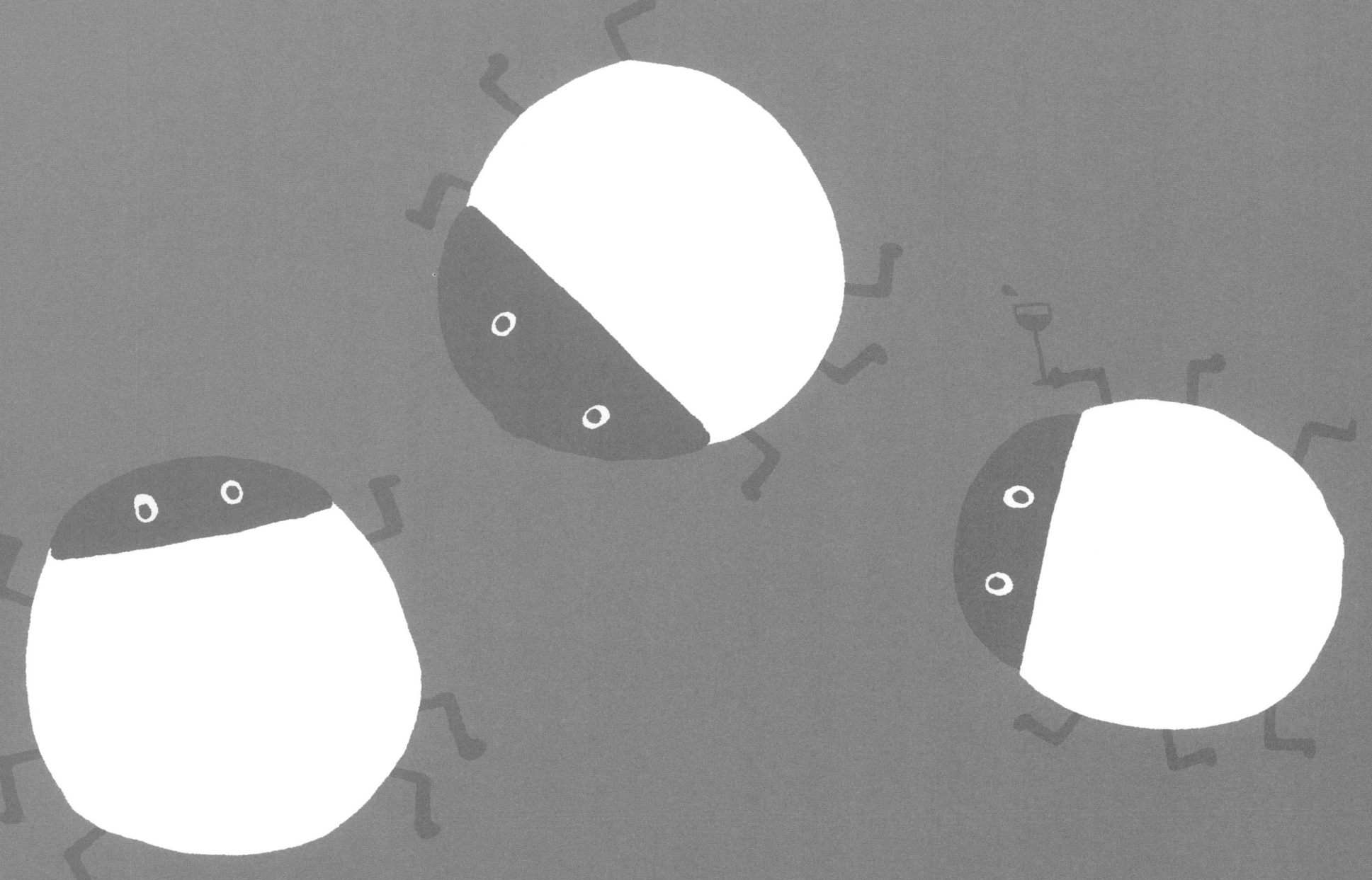

12

How about this long-necked dinosaur?
Should he be one color? Many colors? Patterned?
You decide!

Why are all these birds here? What are they doing?

What should this long, long, long, long snake look like?
Is he going somewhere?

17

Do you want to color the butterflies?

What about the flowers?

It's an animal costume party!
The kitty is going as a lion.

How should the other animals dress up?

What would all these faces look like with lipstick?

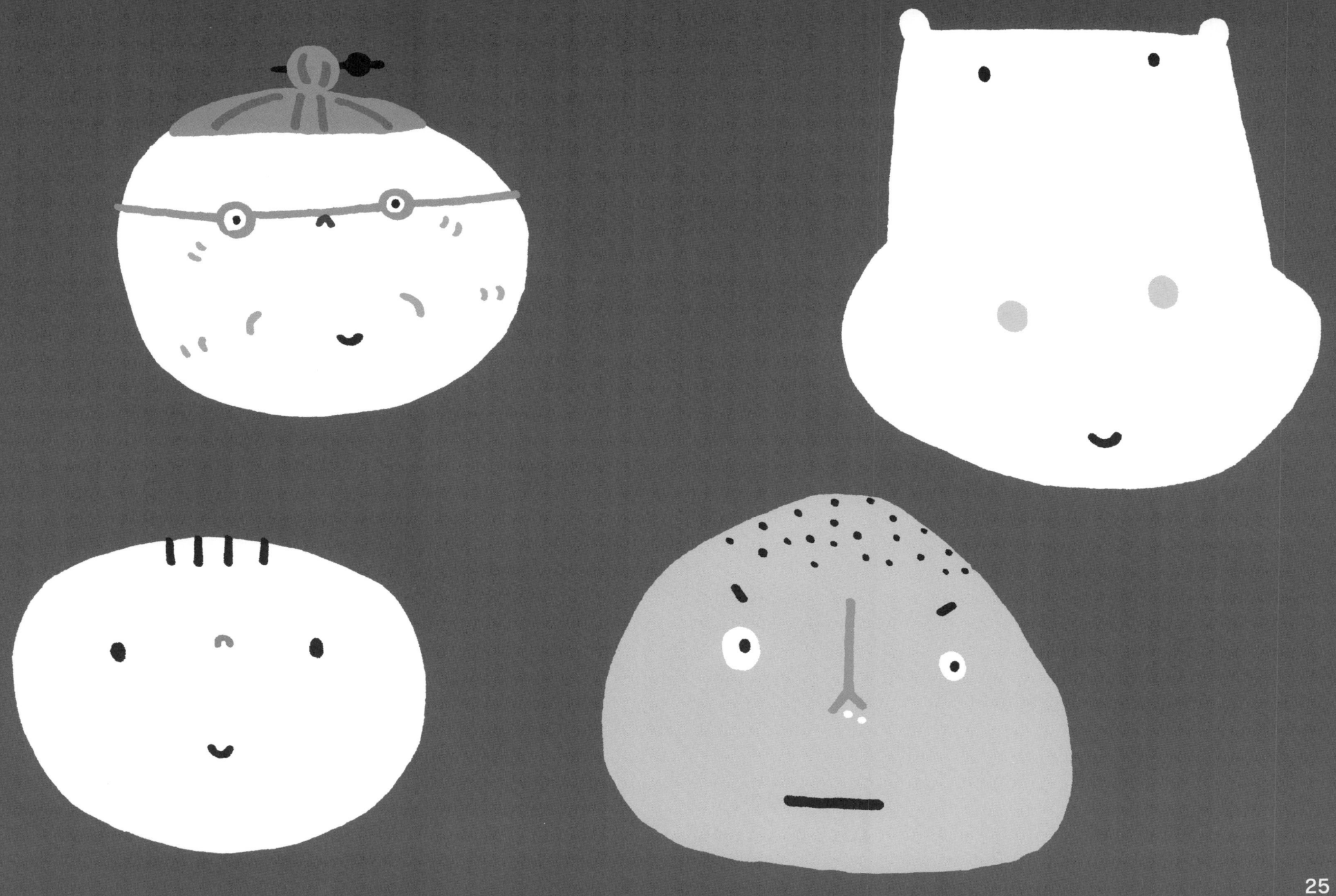

Let's color in the patterns on their dresses.

Should we color in the socks or give them stripes?

Let's liven up these hats.

Let's make this hat extra fancy.

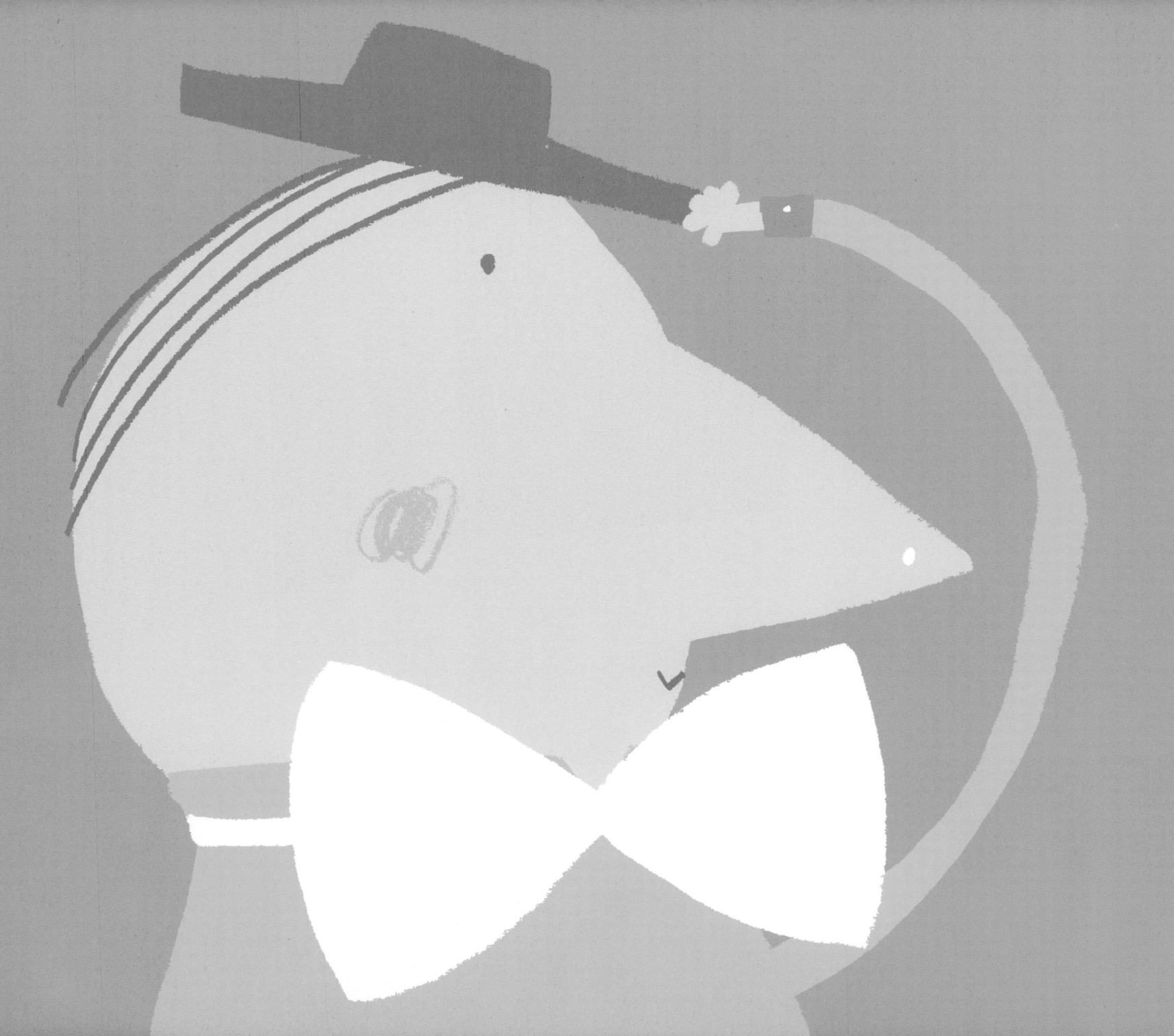

Decorate the bow ties.

Please give all of us bow ties.

We'd like bow ties too!

This house is all alone. How can you change that?

Try using a white crayon on this page.

Let's draw faces and clothing on the snowmen.

45

Let's give some colors and stripes to the fish.

Name and decorate this enormous ship.

Blow bubbles. Bubble bubble bubble.

Drop drop drop...

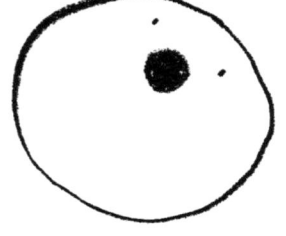

Let's draw friends for the raindrops.

One block became a fish. Another became a train car. Turn all the blocks into something else.

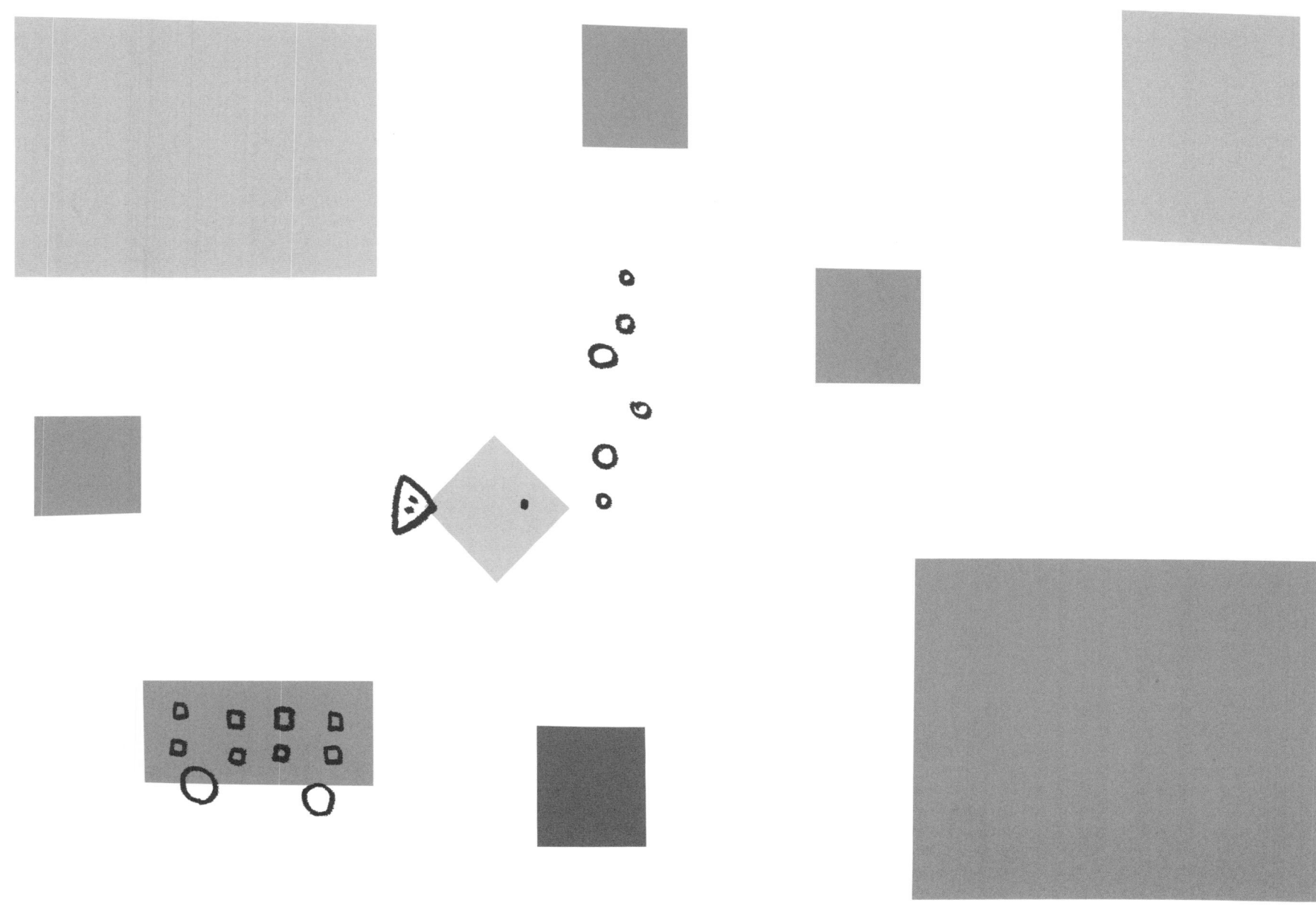

Everyone wants antennae!
Let's put antennae on everyone.

Is there anyone home in these buildings?

Color the lights and decorations.

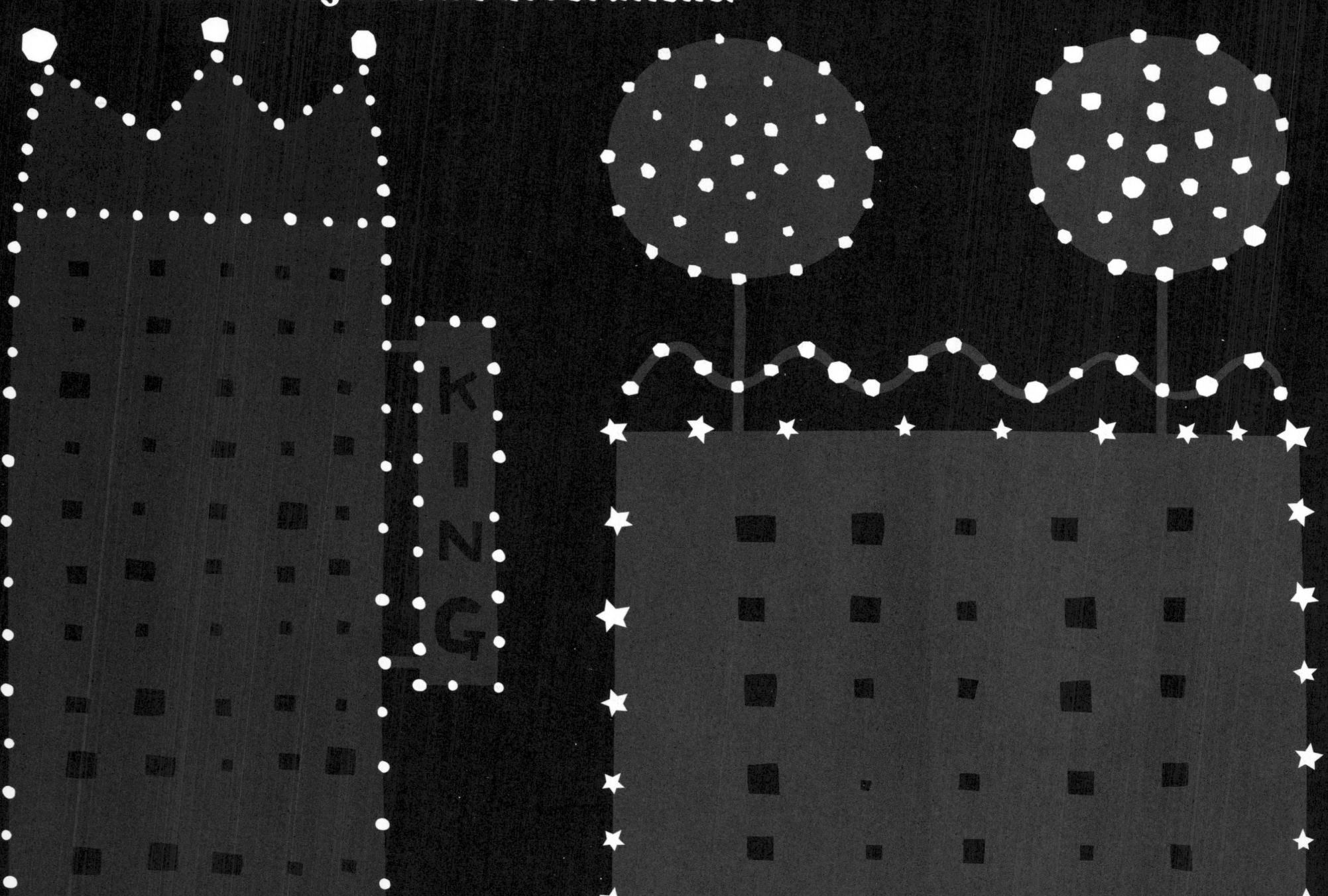

60

What colors do you think you'd find in outer space?

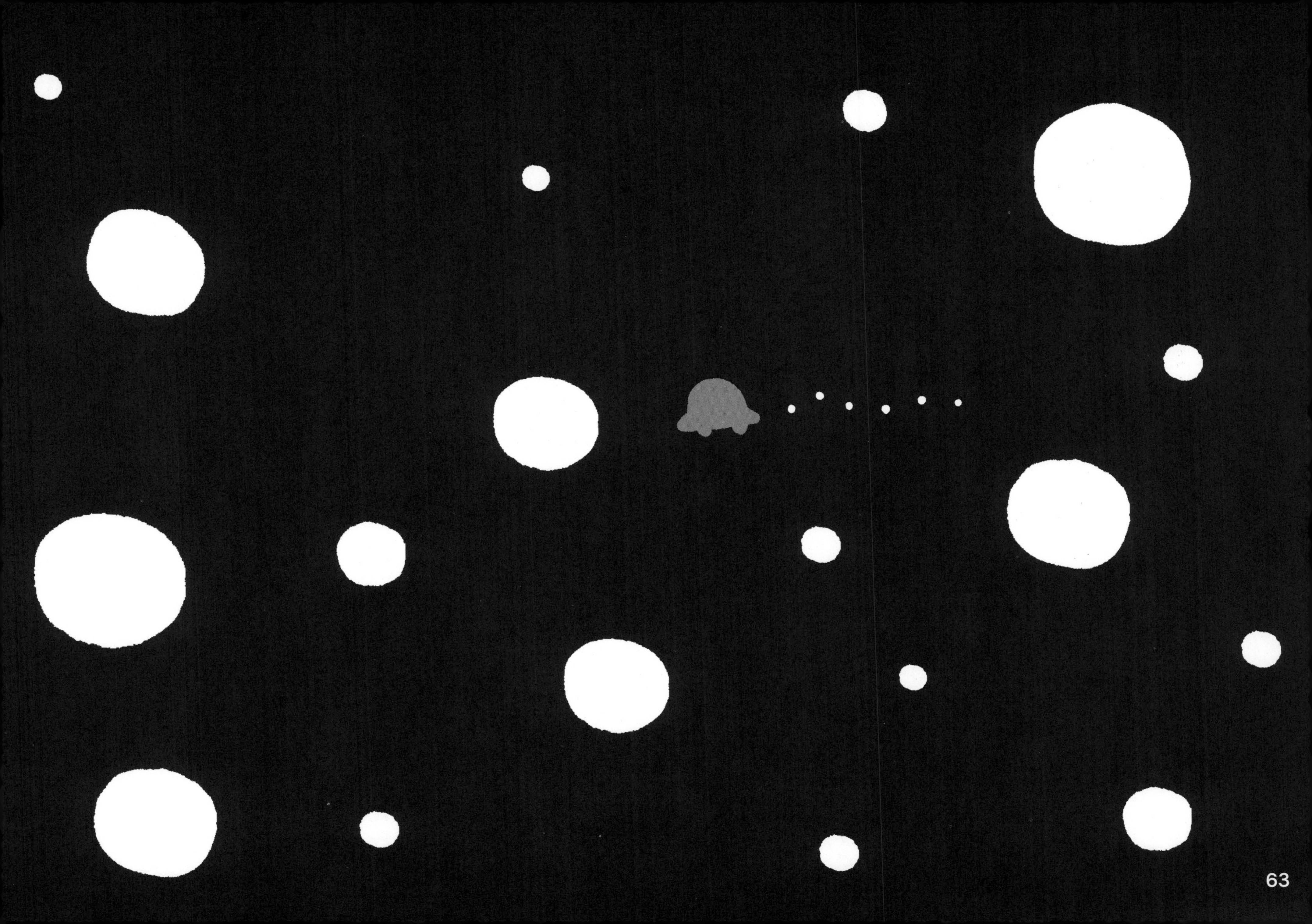

Let's make a storm!

What could these shapes become in outer space?

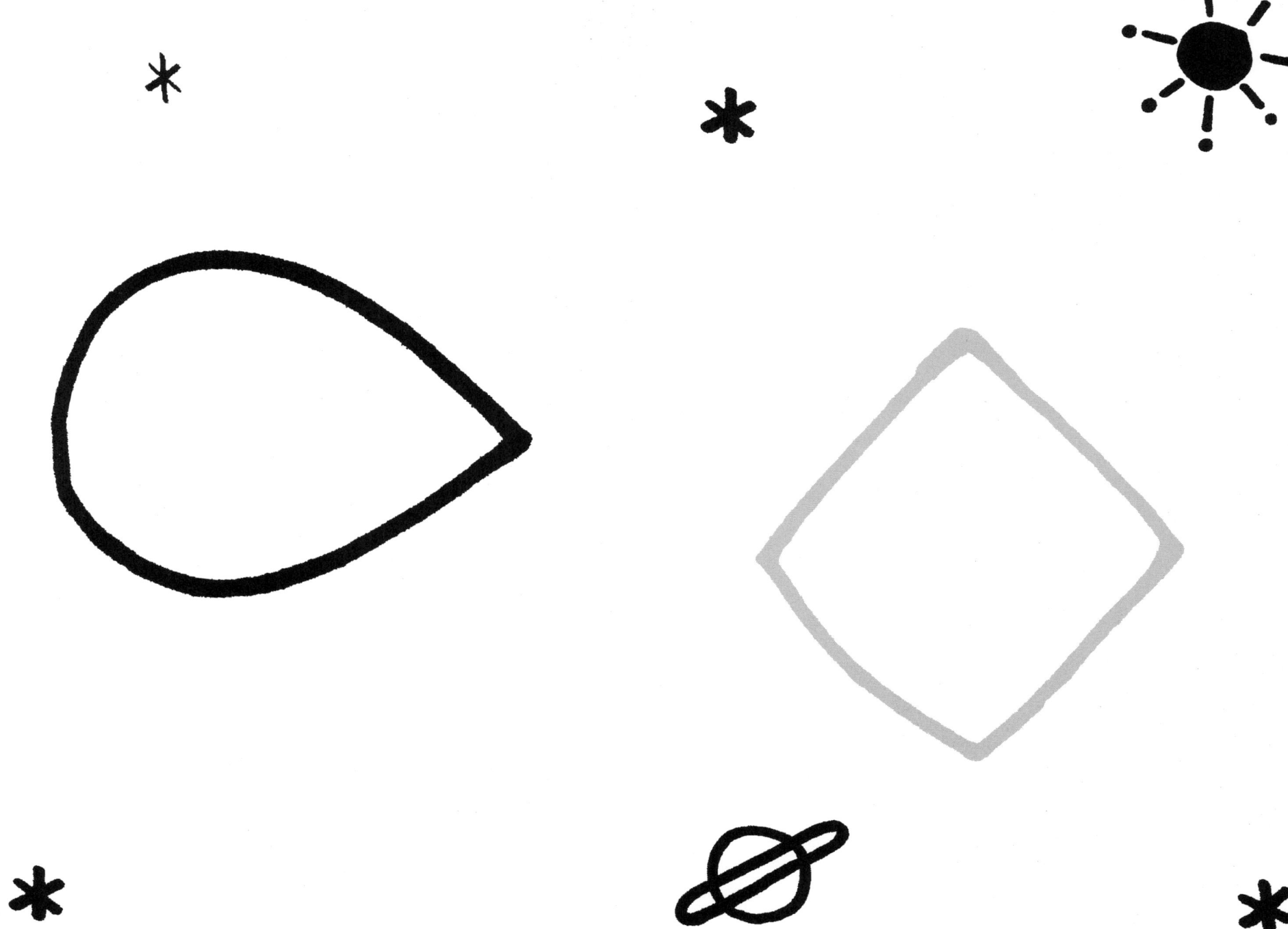

Oh, my!  Oh, goodness!

Zoom!

**Will something come out
of my hat, too?**

Draw faces on all the germs that came out with my sneeze.

What kind of glasses do people wear?

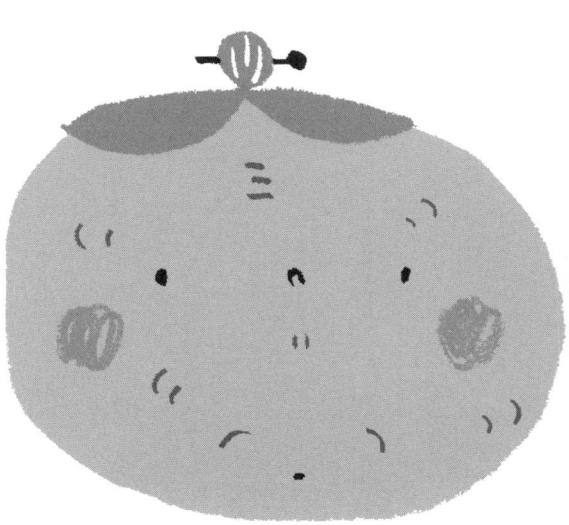

Would it be silly to give an elephant glasses?

Or a lion? Let's try it!

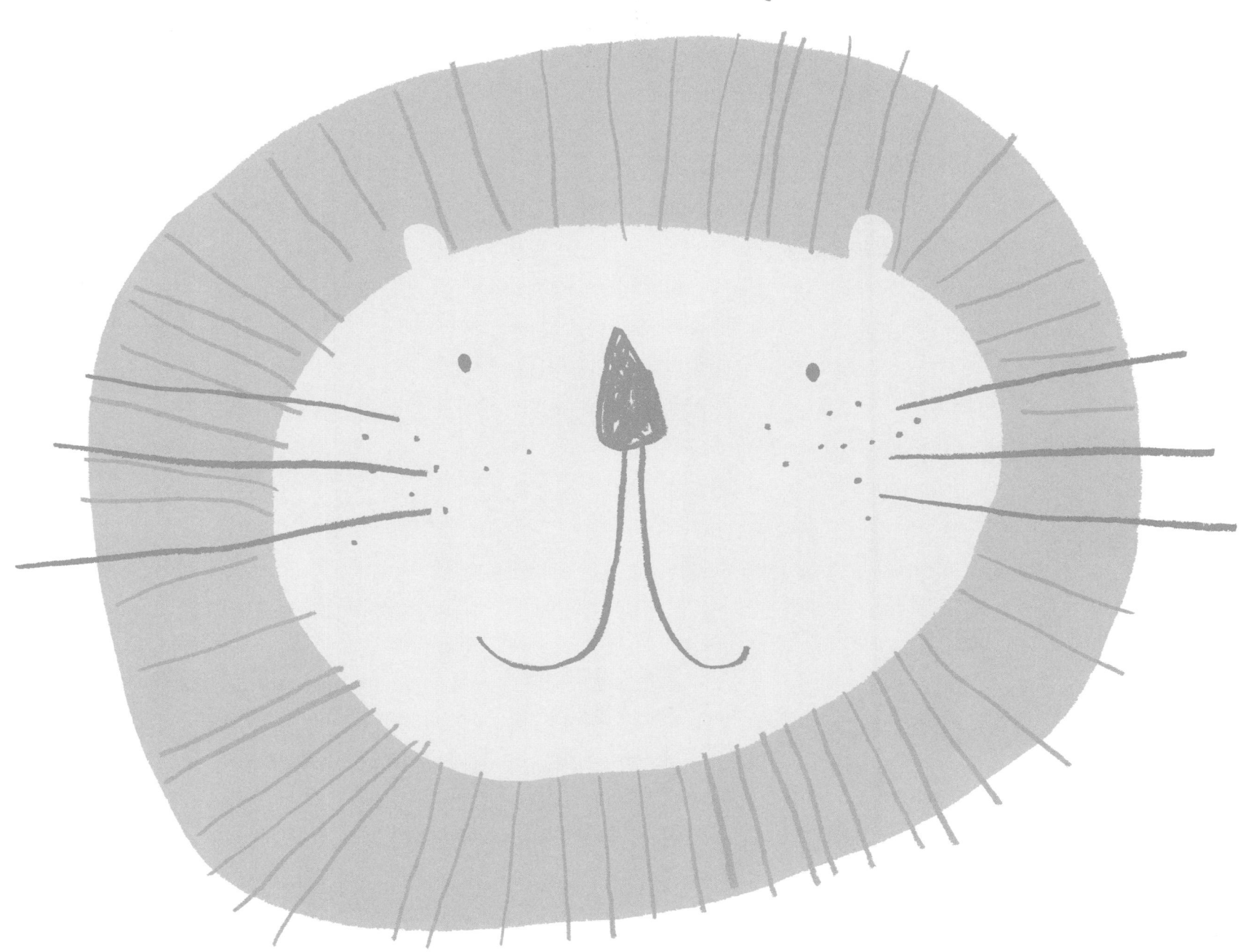

What are these weird shapes?
What colors should they be?

What are these lines? What do you think?

Decorate the cakes.

What are we celebrating?

Let's create an ocean inside the cup.

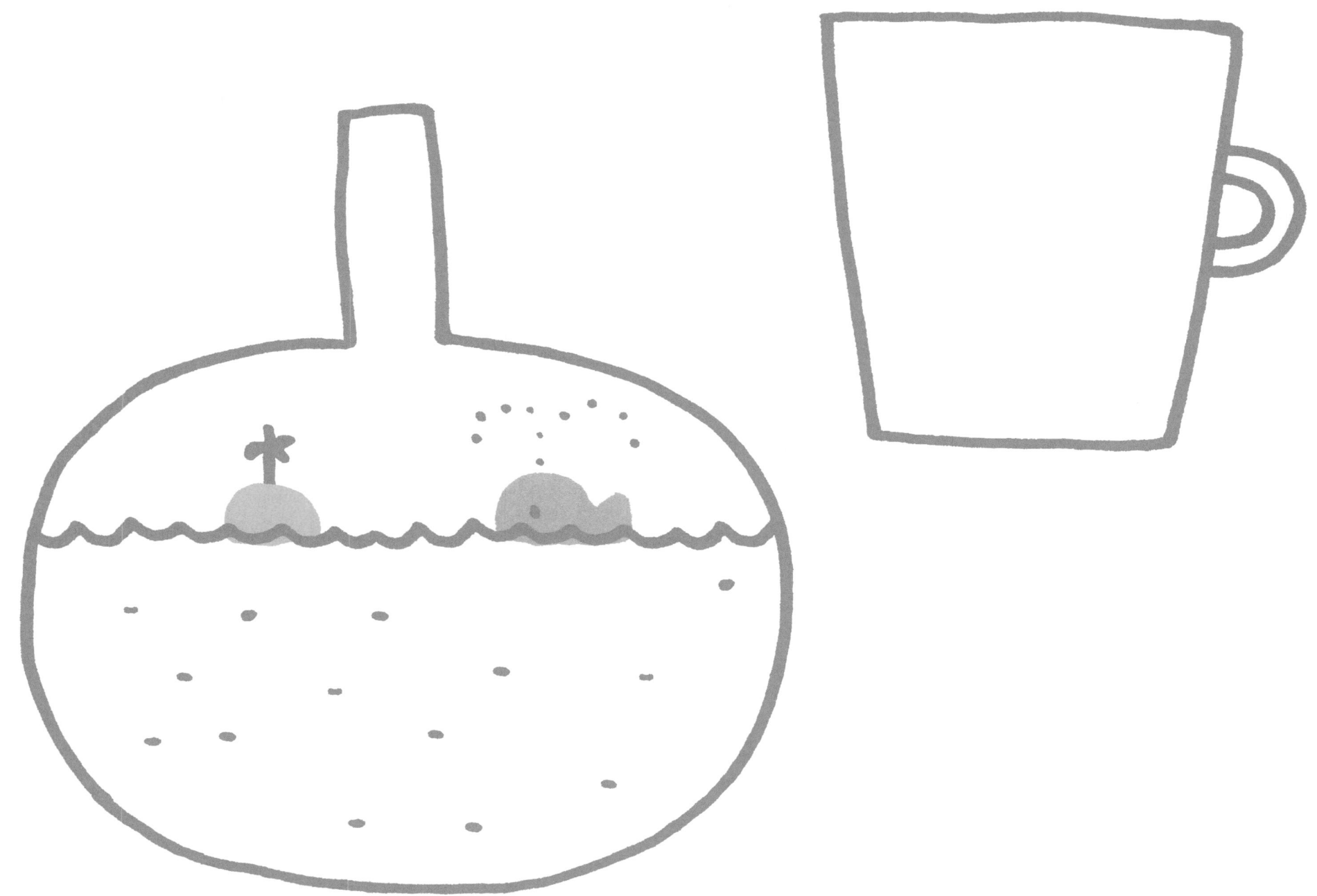

Are there waves, ships, fish?

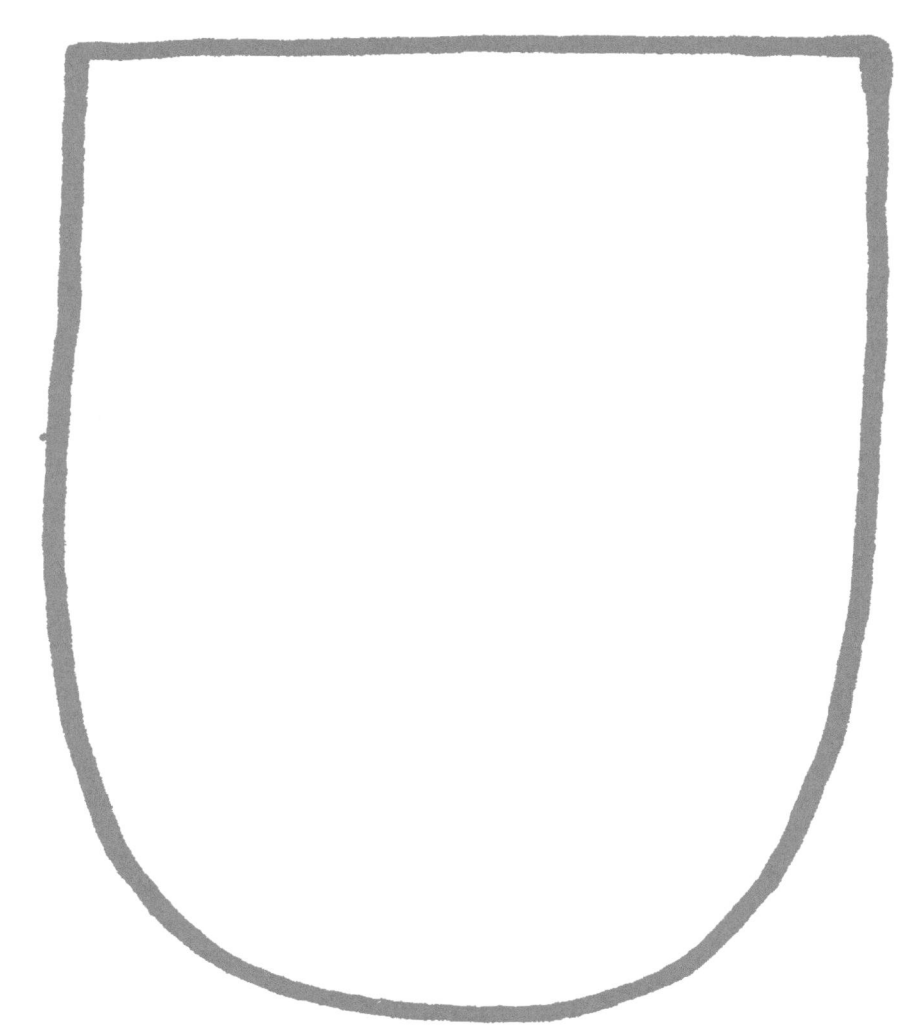

Give them horns or antlers and turn them into imaginary creatures.

What are these eyes missing? Draw them!

How is this boy feeling?
Draw a mouth that shows that emotion.

This girl is happy!
Draw what makes her feel that way.

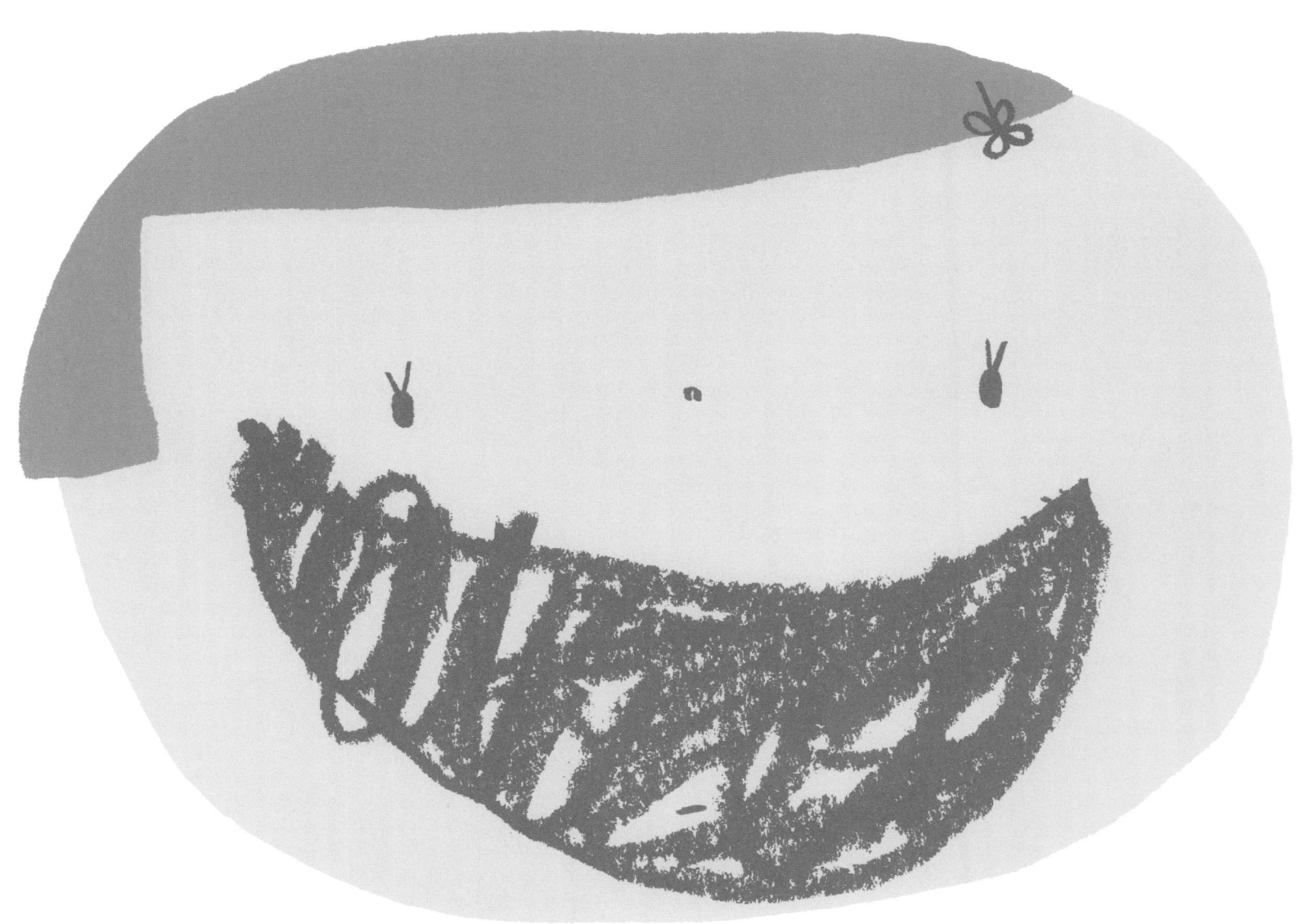

How about these kids? What are they feeling?

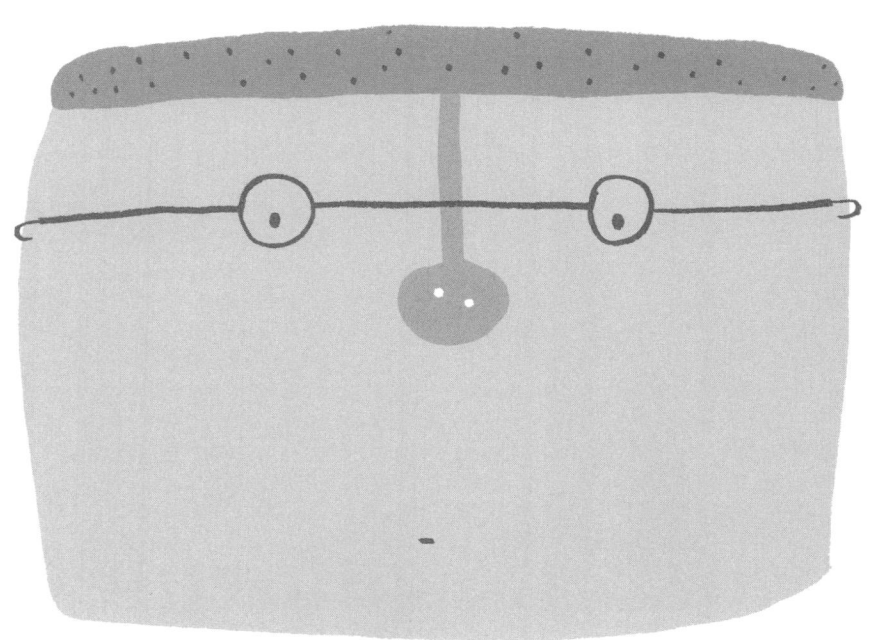

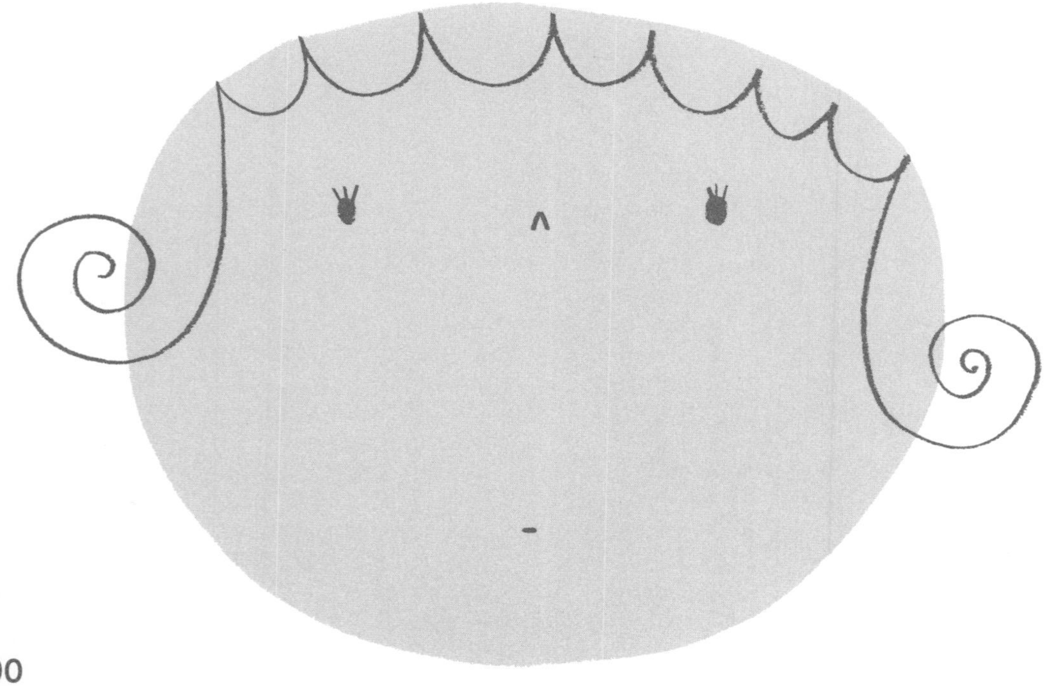

And their grandpa and grandma? How about them?

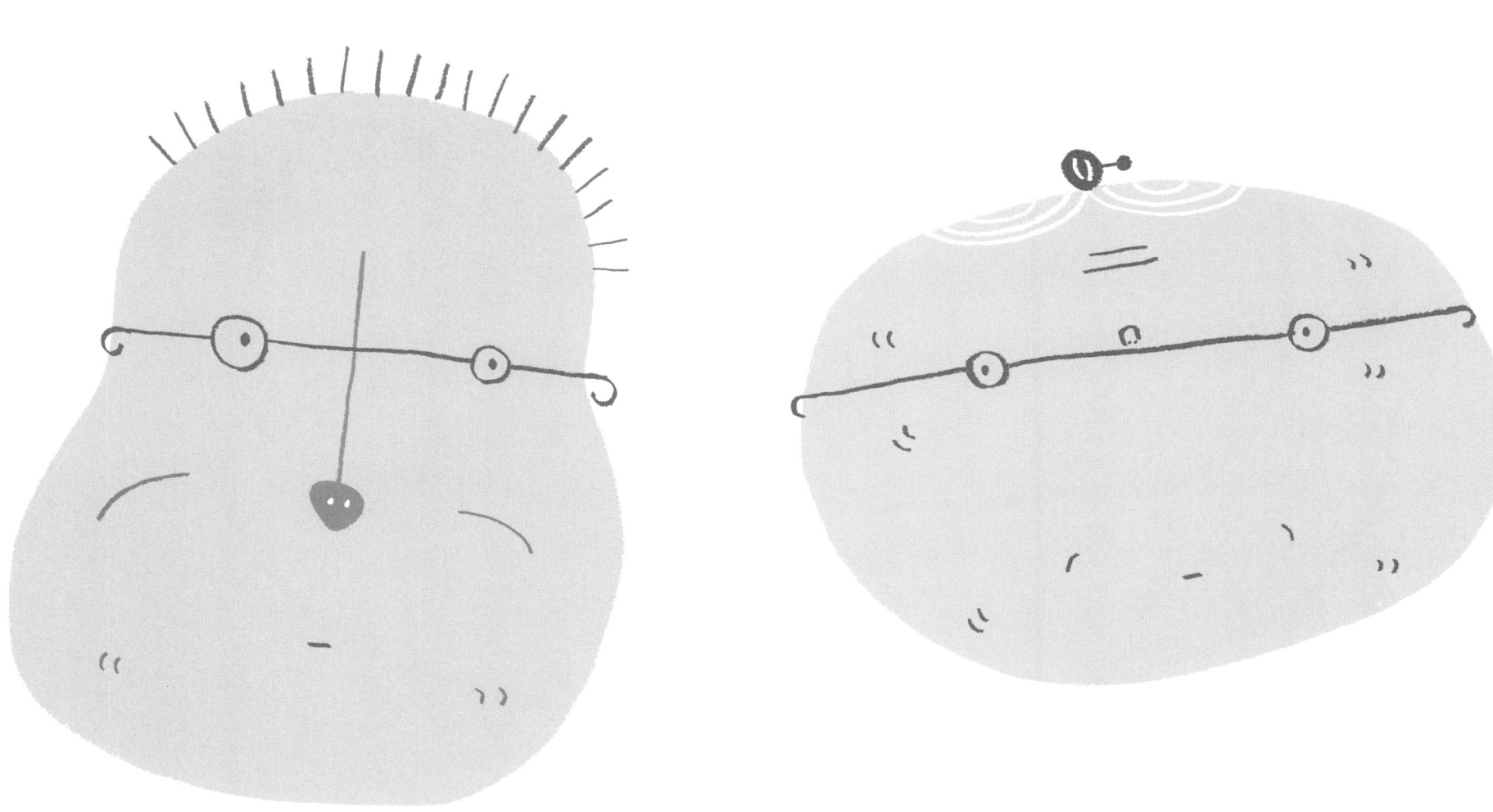

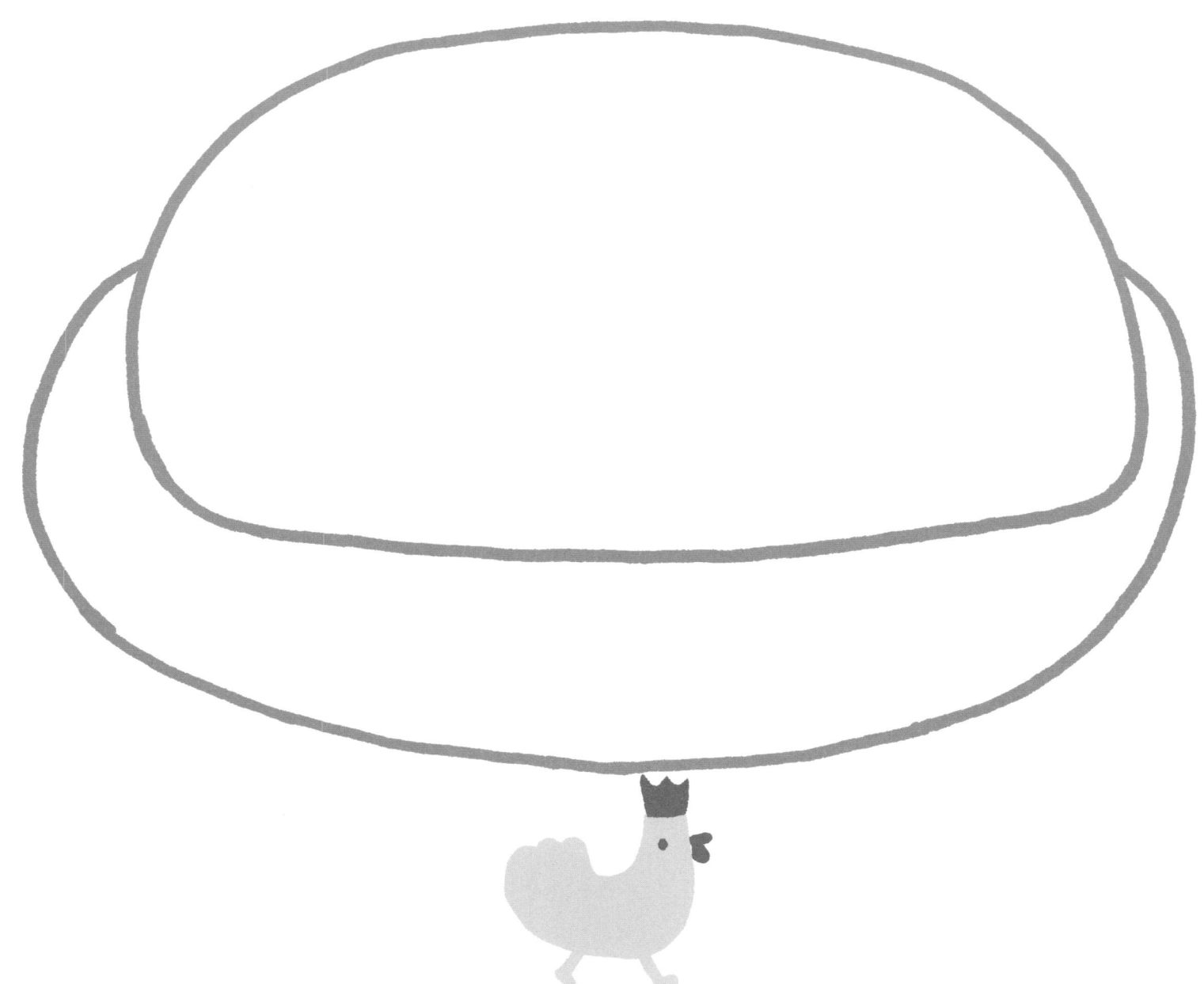

Help these boys finish getting ready for the party!

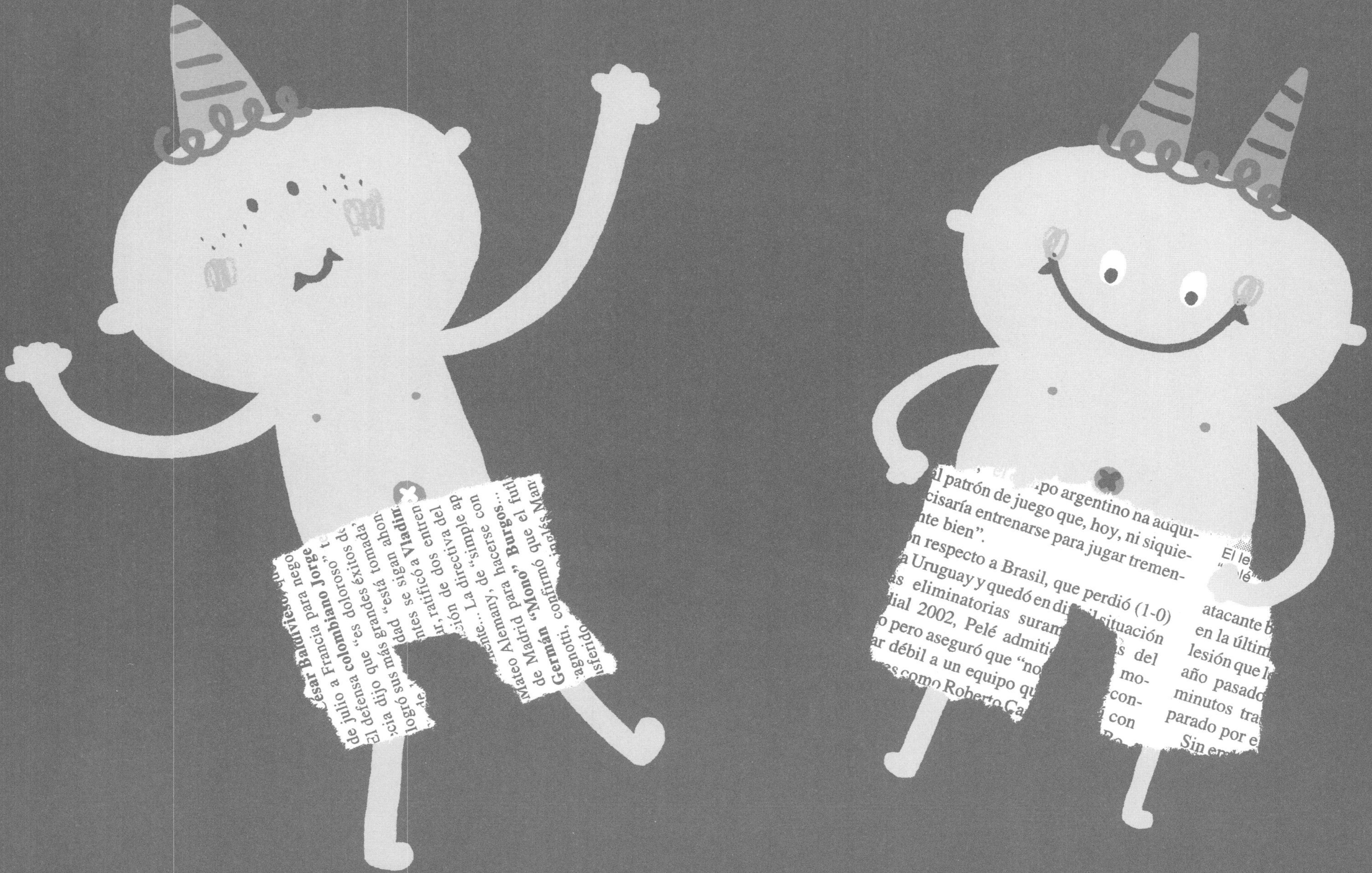

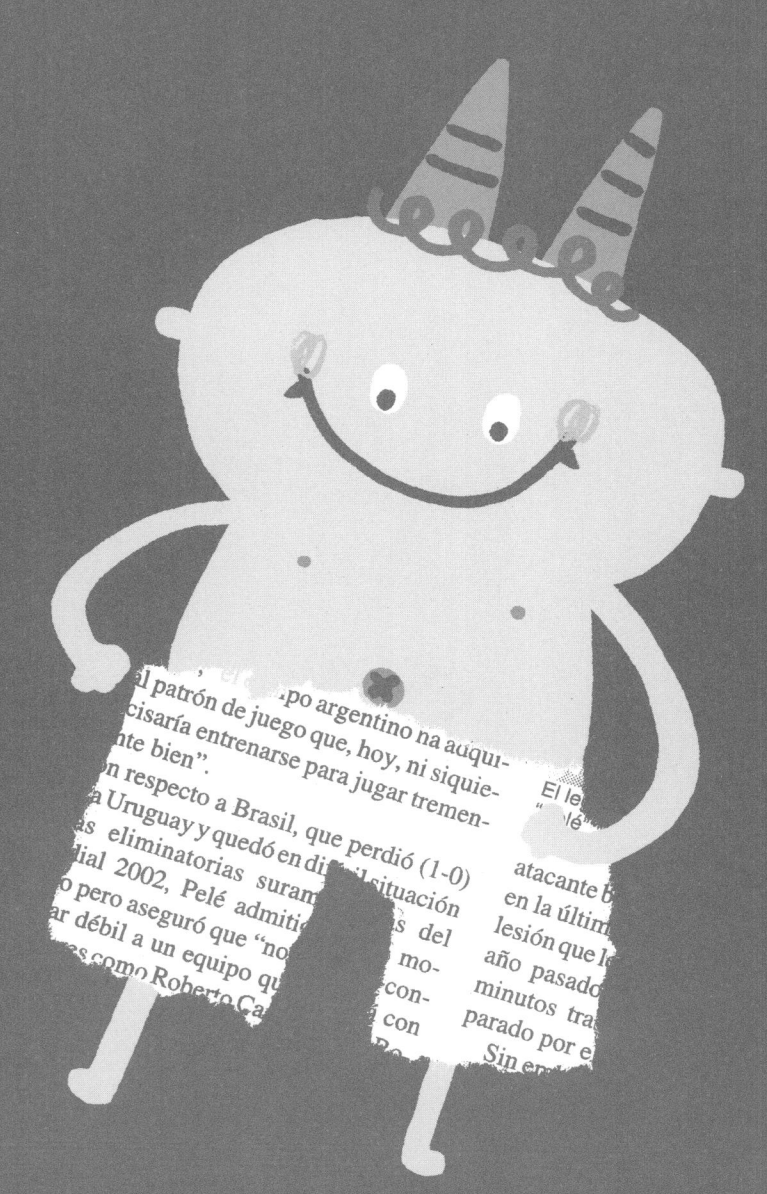

Many things can grow on trees.
What kind of tree can you imagine?

A heart tree?

A sun tree?

Is it hot here
or just me?

Can you finish this car tree?

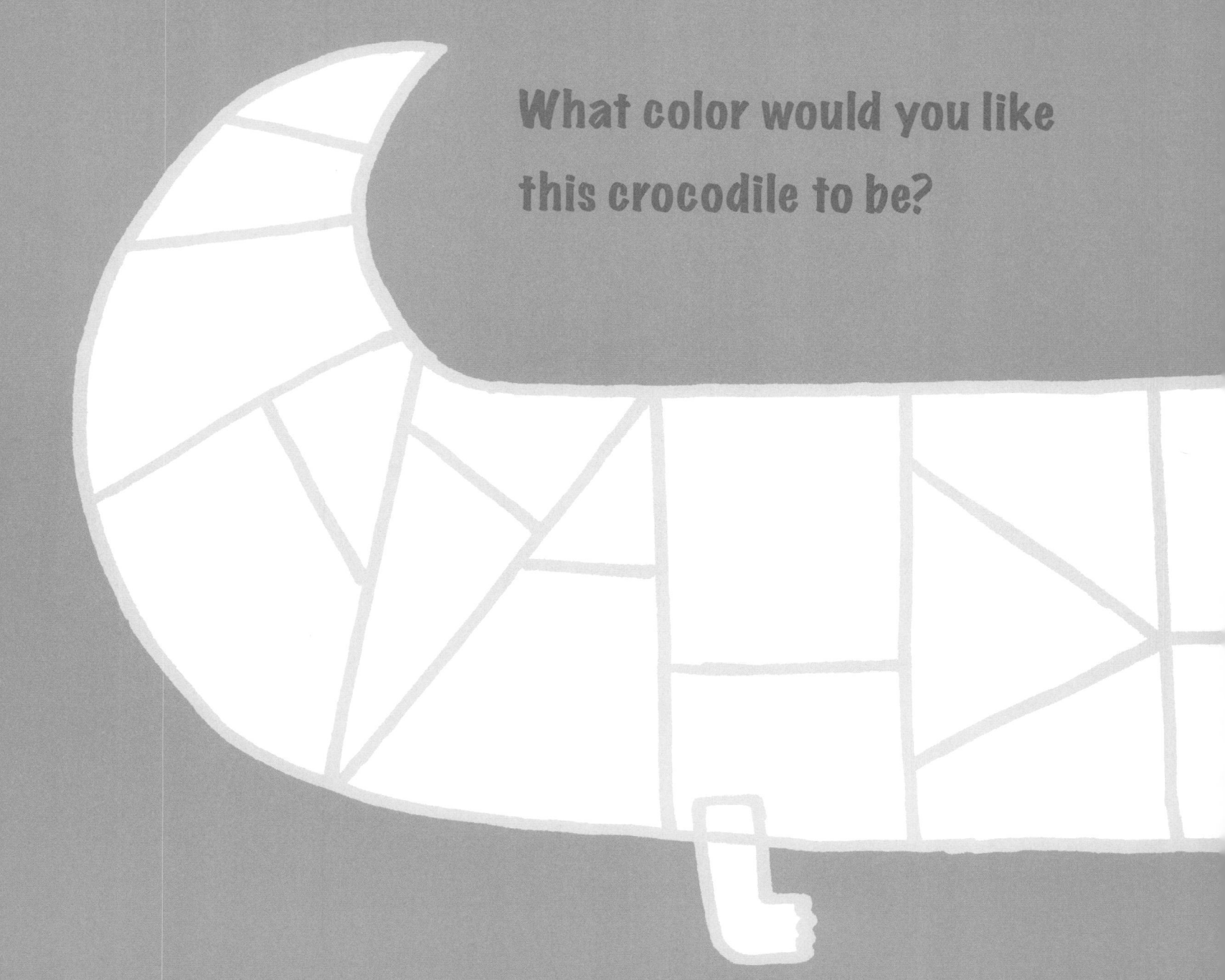

What color would you like
this crocodile to be?

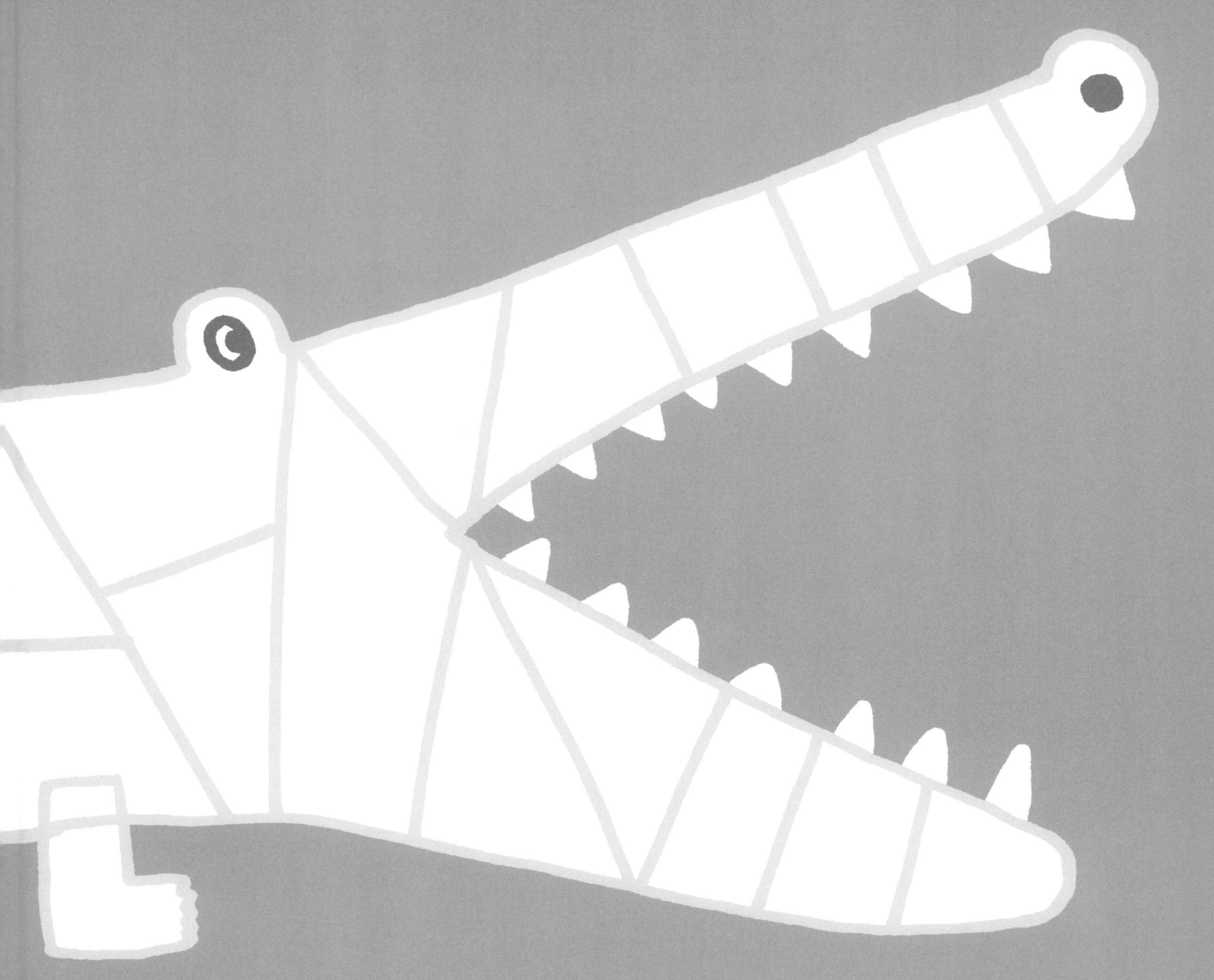

This page has only one lonely elephant on it.

How will you change that?

Give stripes to the snakes.

Hi,
Ms. Stripes!

Hi,
Mr. Stripes!

105

This cloud has a face. What else can happen in the sky?

Are these clouds? Or marshmallow people?
What should they wear?

Let's put different designs on each plane.

**Color the jet plane.
Where is it going?**

Now color the sailboats.

Who else is playing with this whale and his friends?

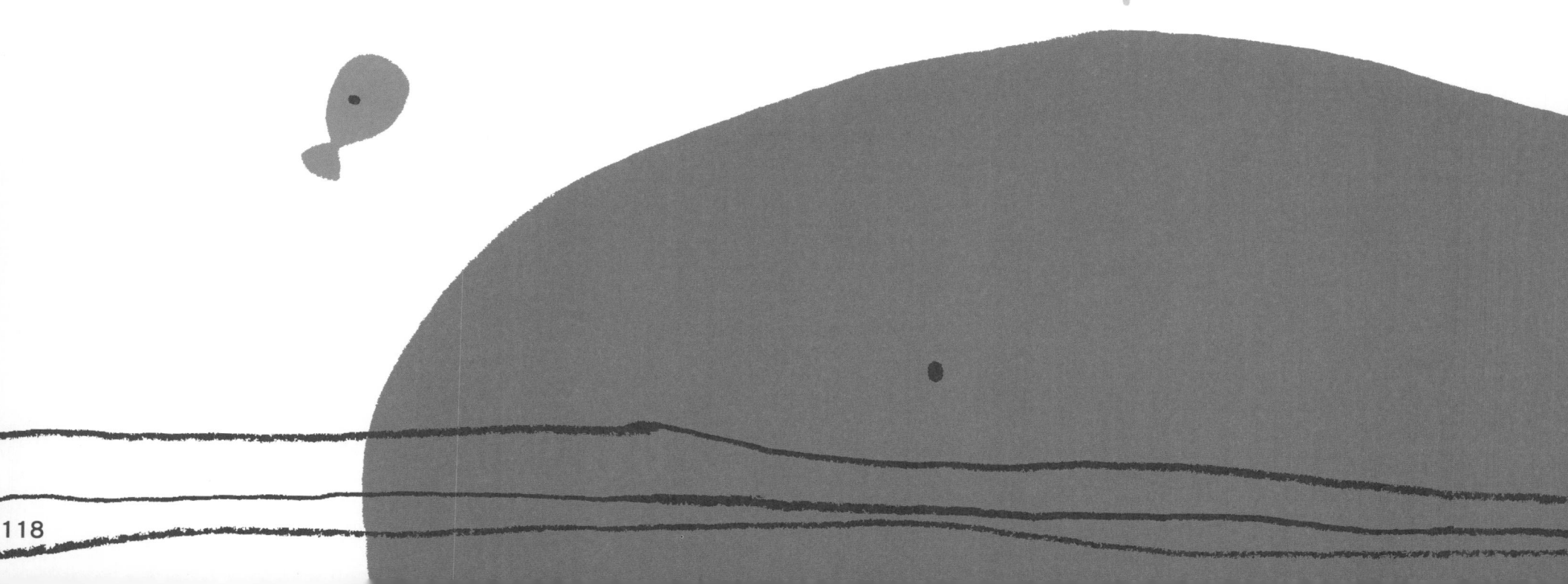

Why is the elephant is taking a shower?

**Should the ant
take a shower, too?**

Butterflies love flowers.

What kind of butterflies can you imagine?

What's going on with these houses?
Is it nighttime? Where are the windows?

Here is one flower.

What else could you draw to keep it company?

It's this panda's birthday and everybody wants to look like a panda to surprise him!

Can you help?

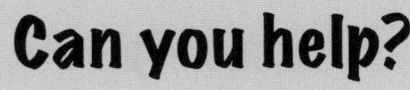

Let's turn all the round shapes into different things.

What are these wacky ghosts doing?

It's a ghost fashion show.
Draw outfits on the ghosts and make them look fancy.

What story can you draw that starts with one ant?

What is the story behind these footprints and paw prints?

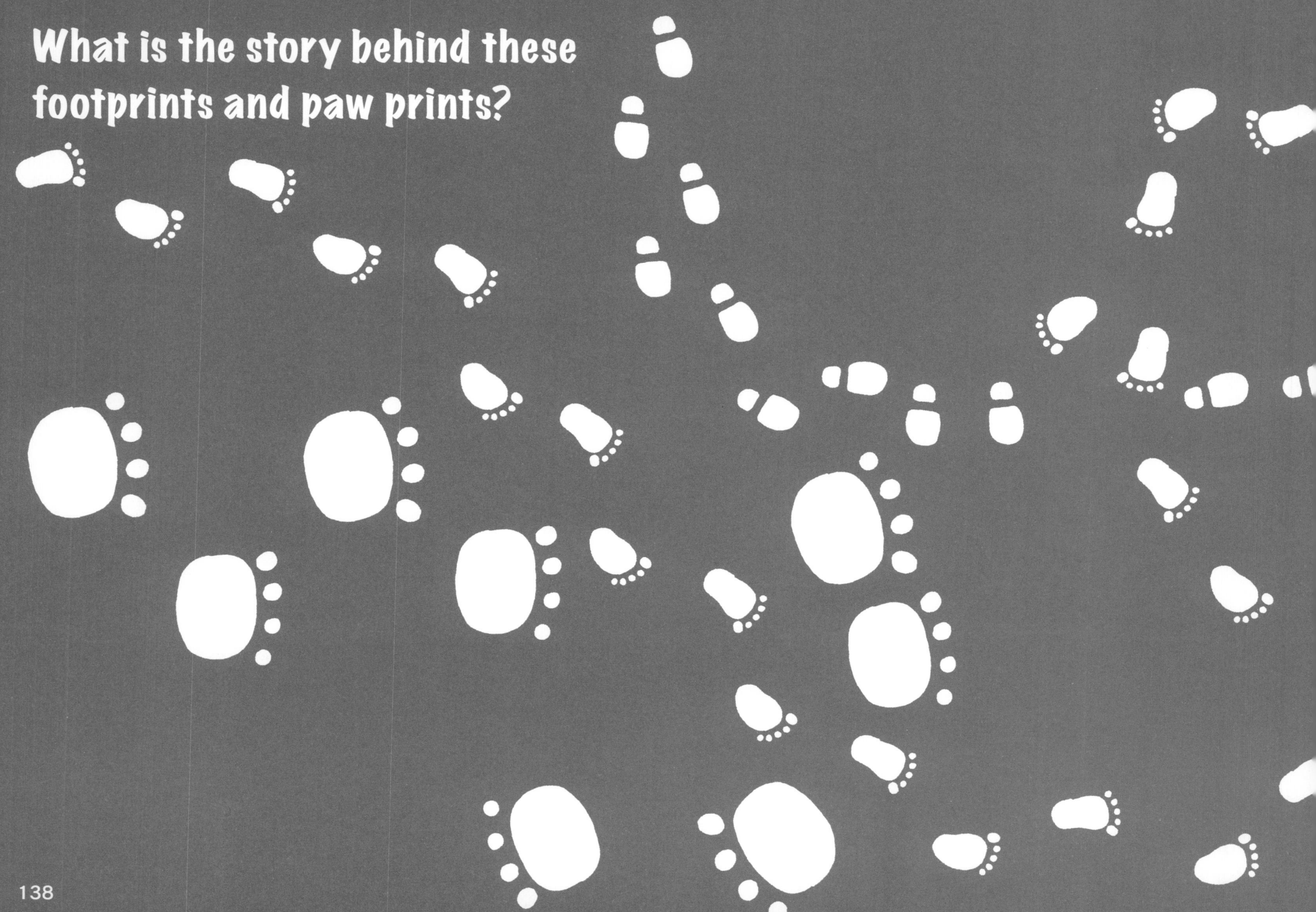

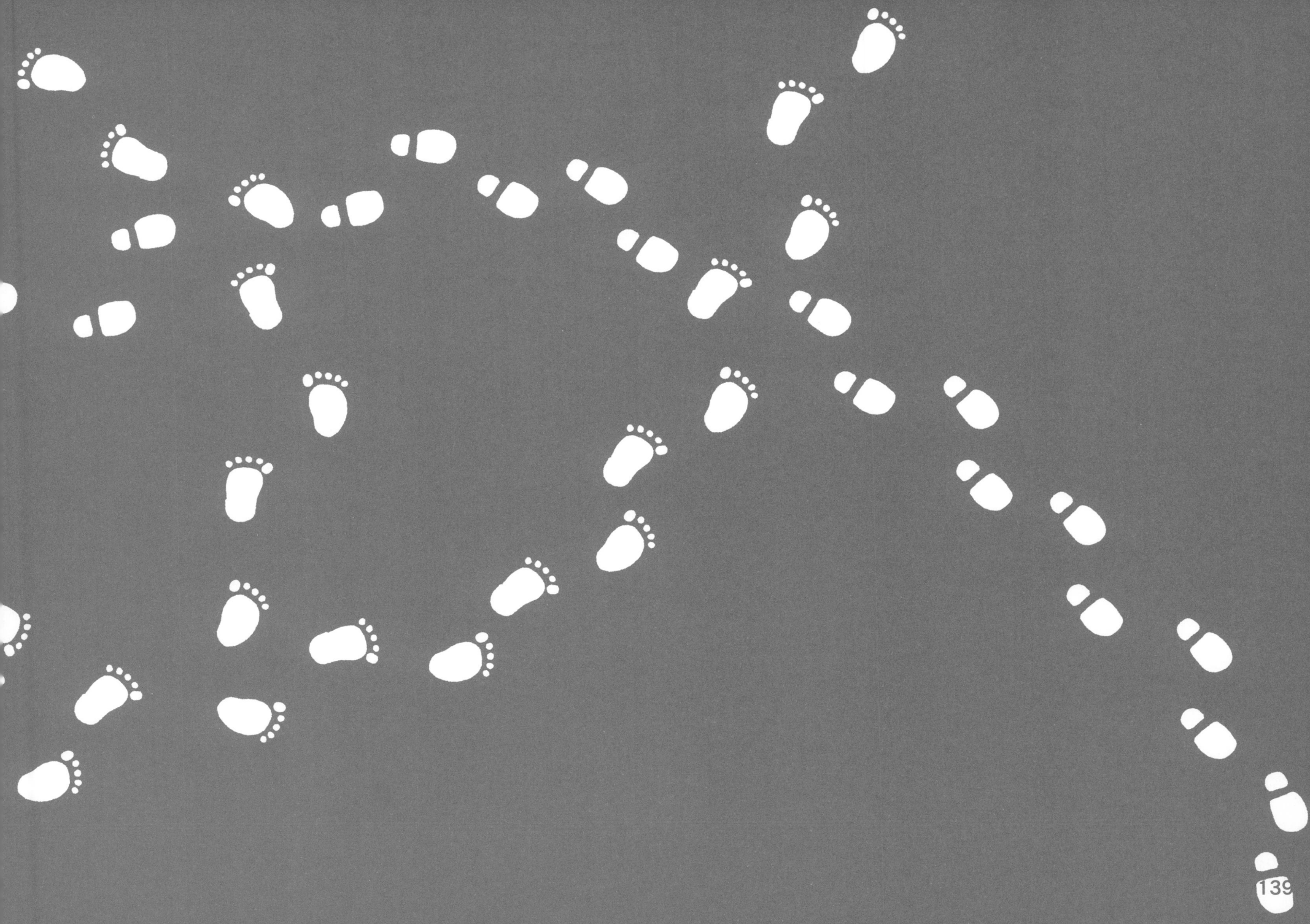

What do you want to draw in the squares?

Are these horses... or zebras?

Should they have riders?

What do you want to draw in these shapes?

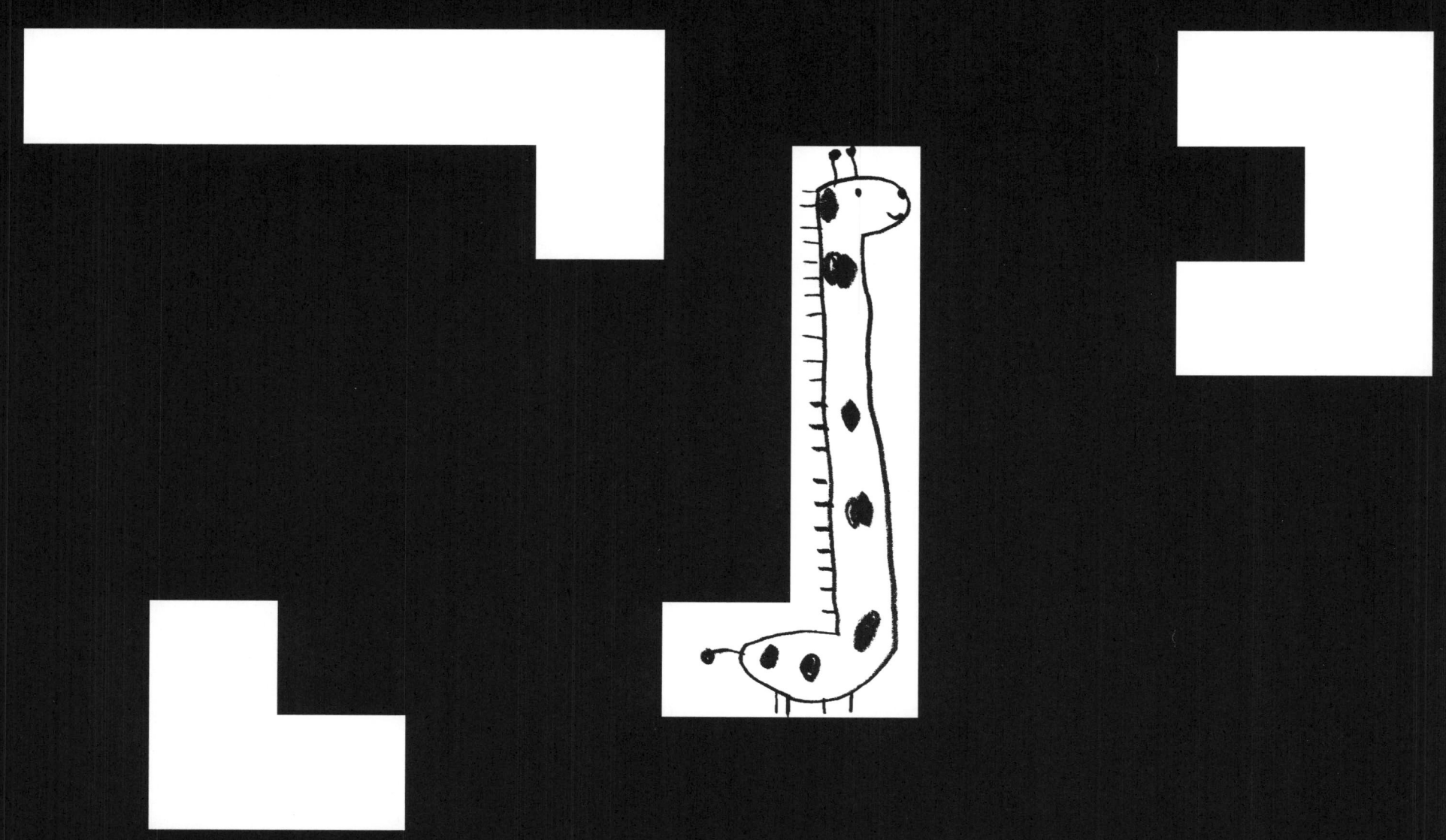

Make this a funny bug.

Can you give him a family?

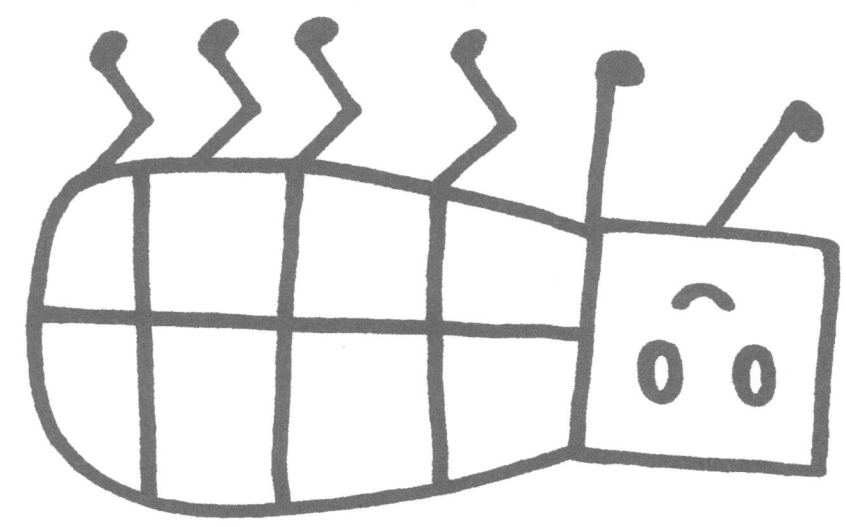

Let's draw faces on these shapes and turn them into strange creatures.

Let's give everyone loooong sticky tongues like a chameleon.

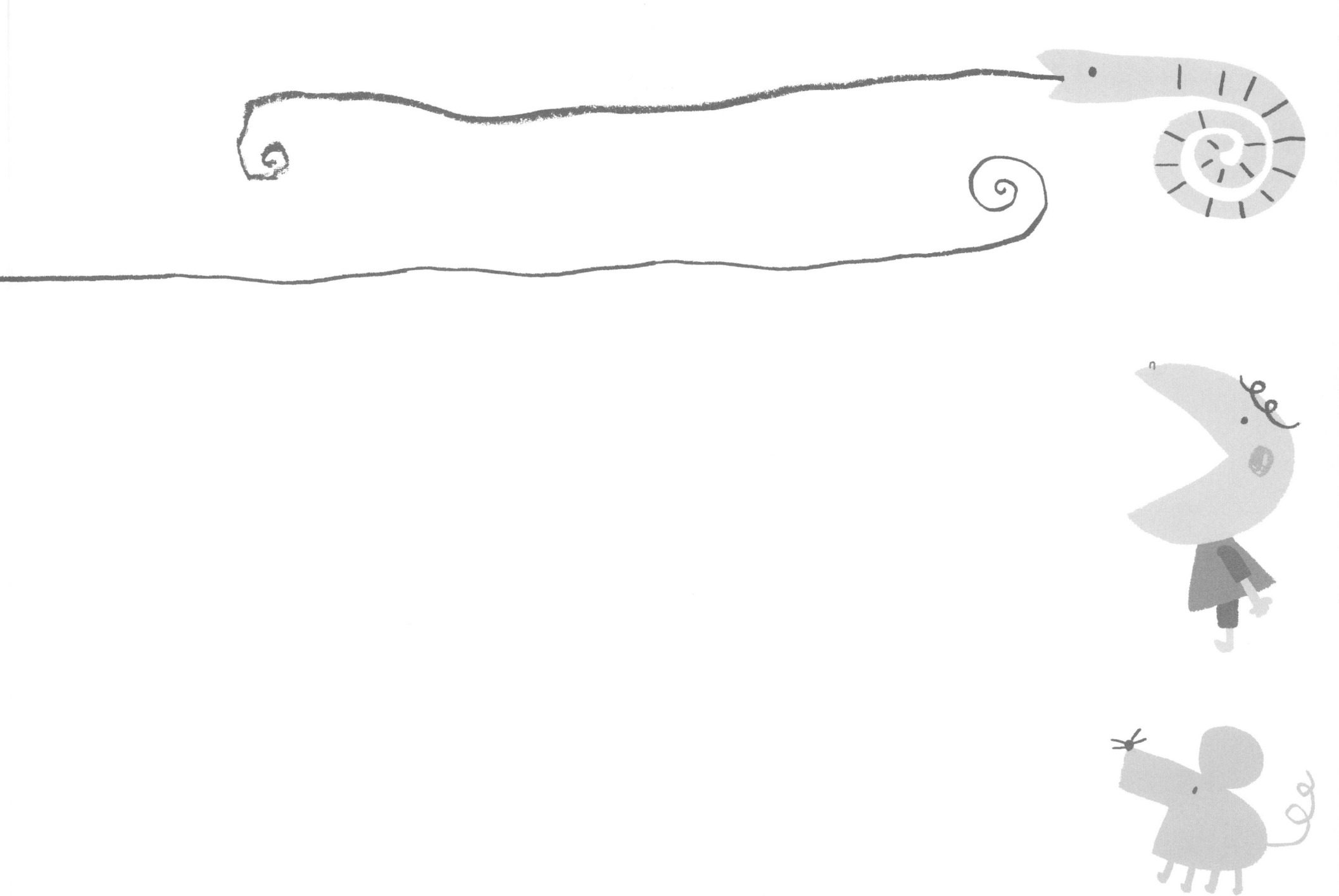

Let's give fluffy wool to the sheep.

153

Let's color the fish.

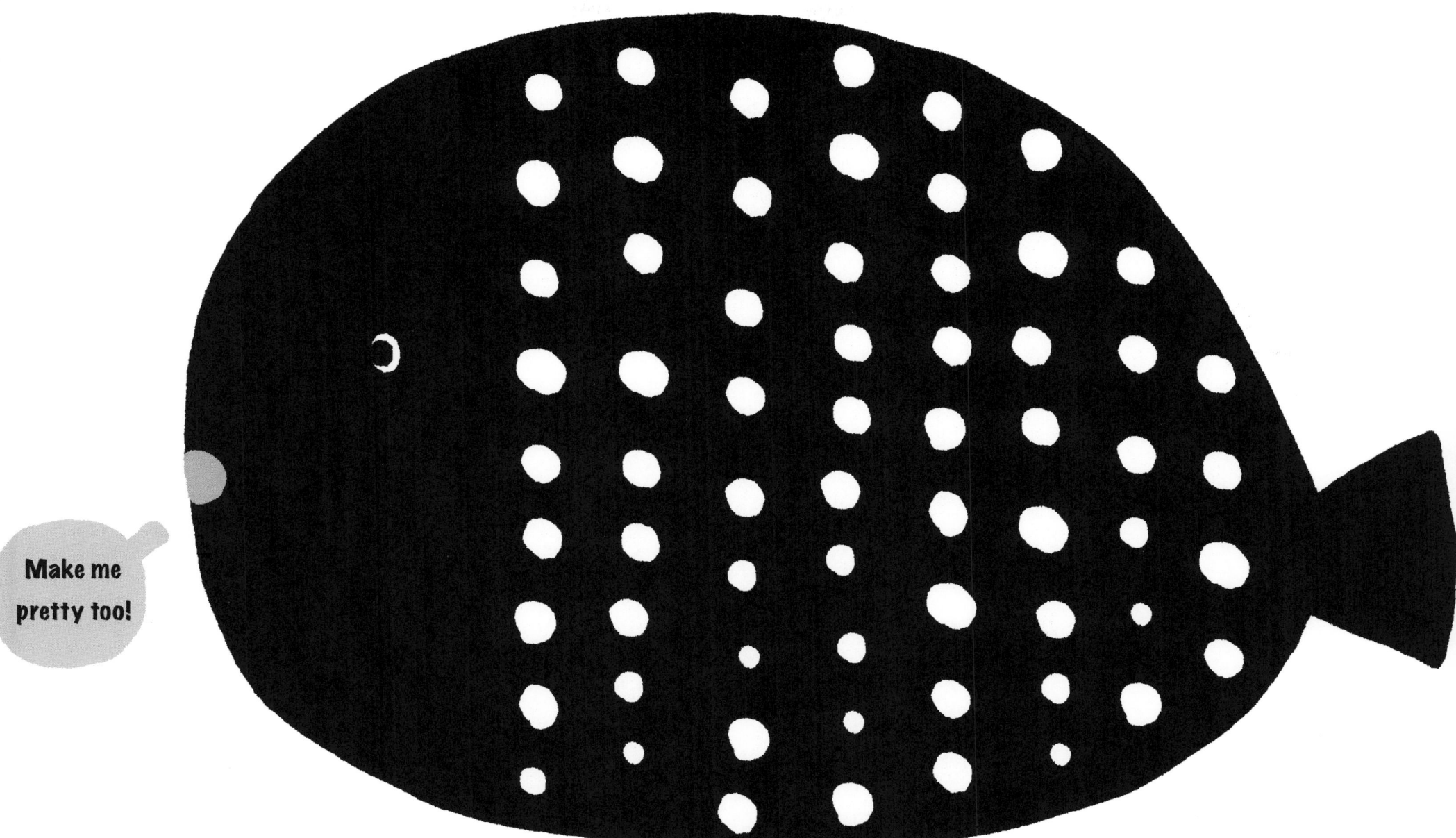

155

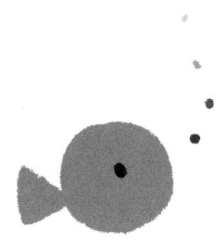

One fish... Where is he? Where is he going?

Draw what you think!

Who are these guys?

What are they doing?

Let's draw roads for the cars.

Welcome home!

What is this? What can you turn it into?

How about this one?

Make all the triangular shapes into something else.

What's going on here?

Draw what you think!

What do you think is traveling on this winding road?

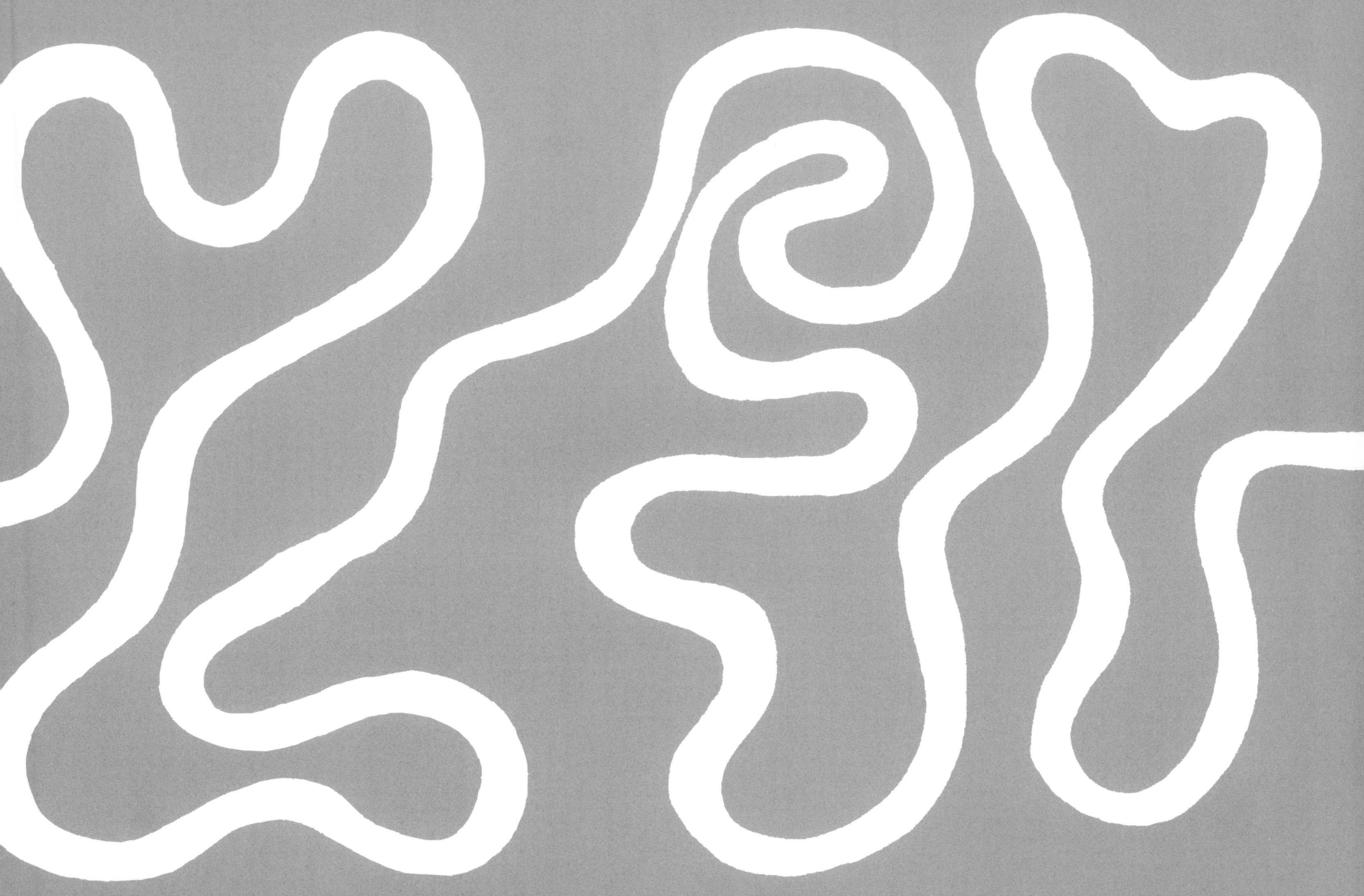

This spider has a web.
Is there anything else in it?

This spider has no web. Can you help out?

Who is traveling on these wacky roads?

This spider wants to be a fashion designer.
Let's make some spider clothing for the elephant...

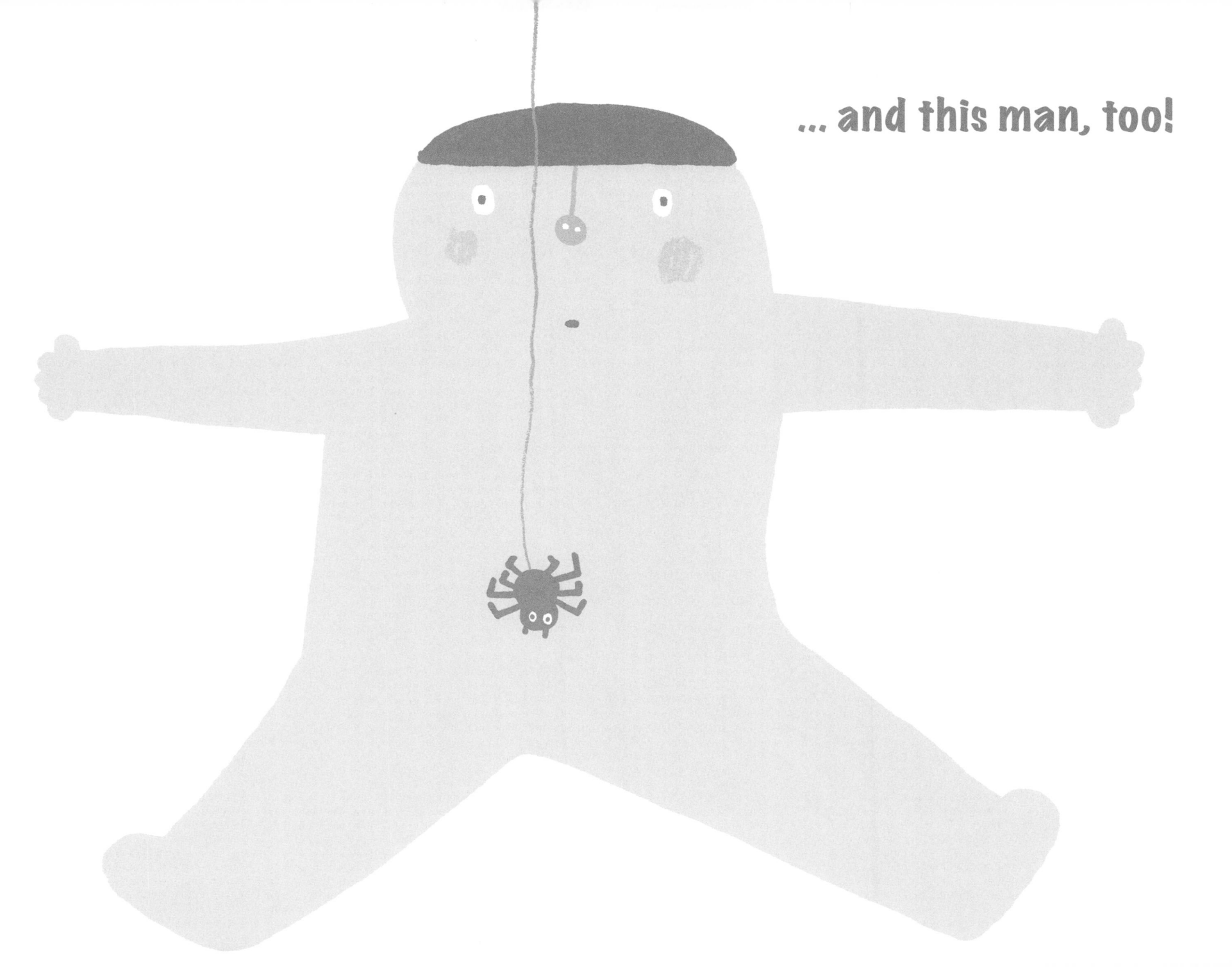

... and this man, too!

Who is traveling on this twisty road?

Let's drive on the whirly road.

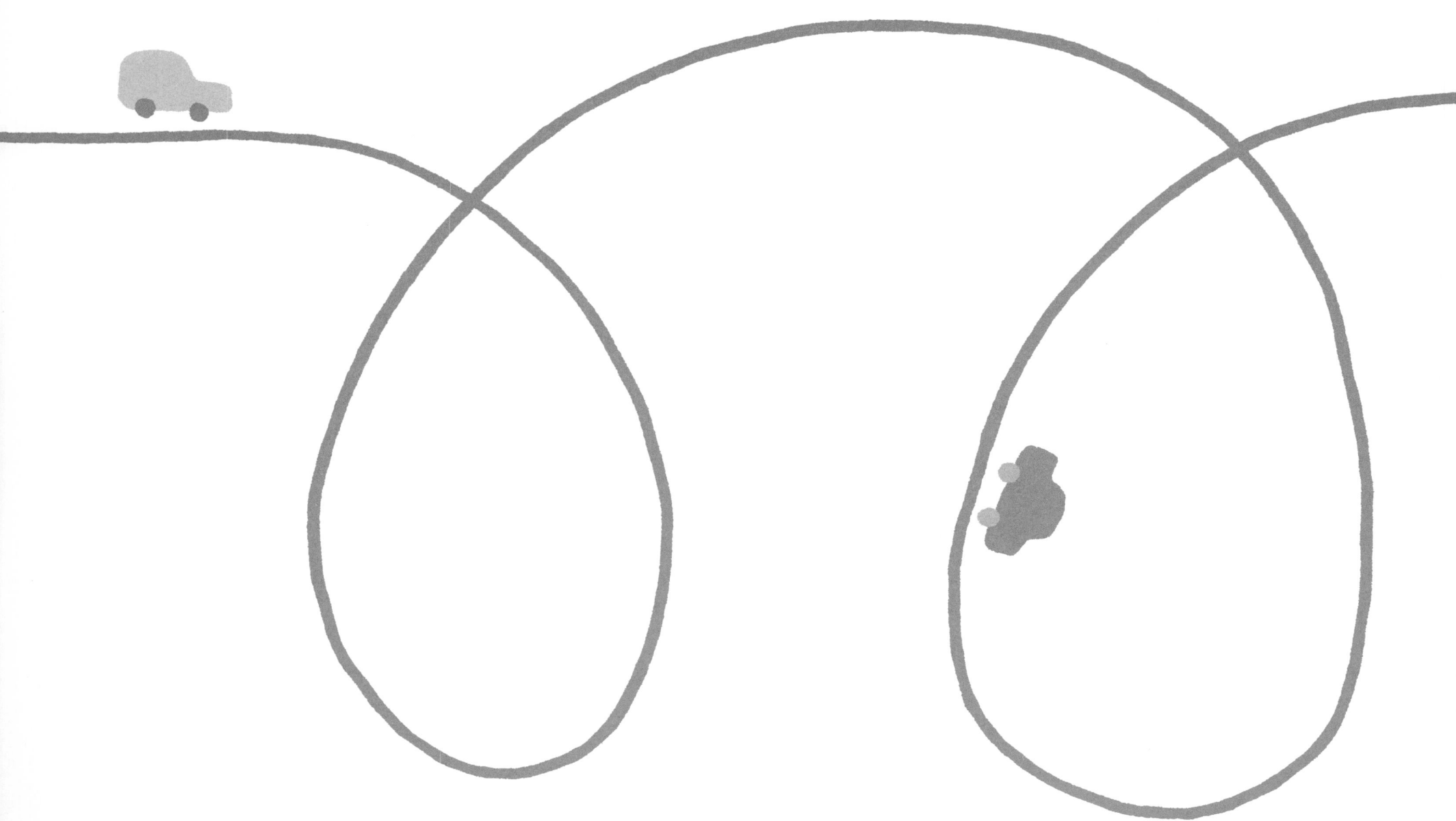

Should there be more traffic?

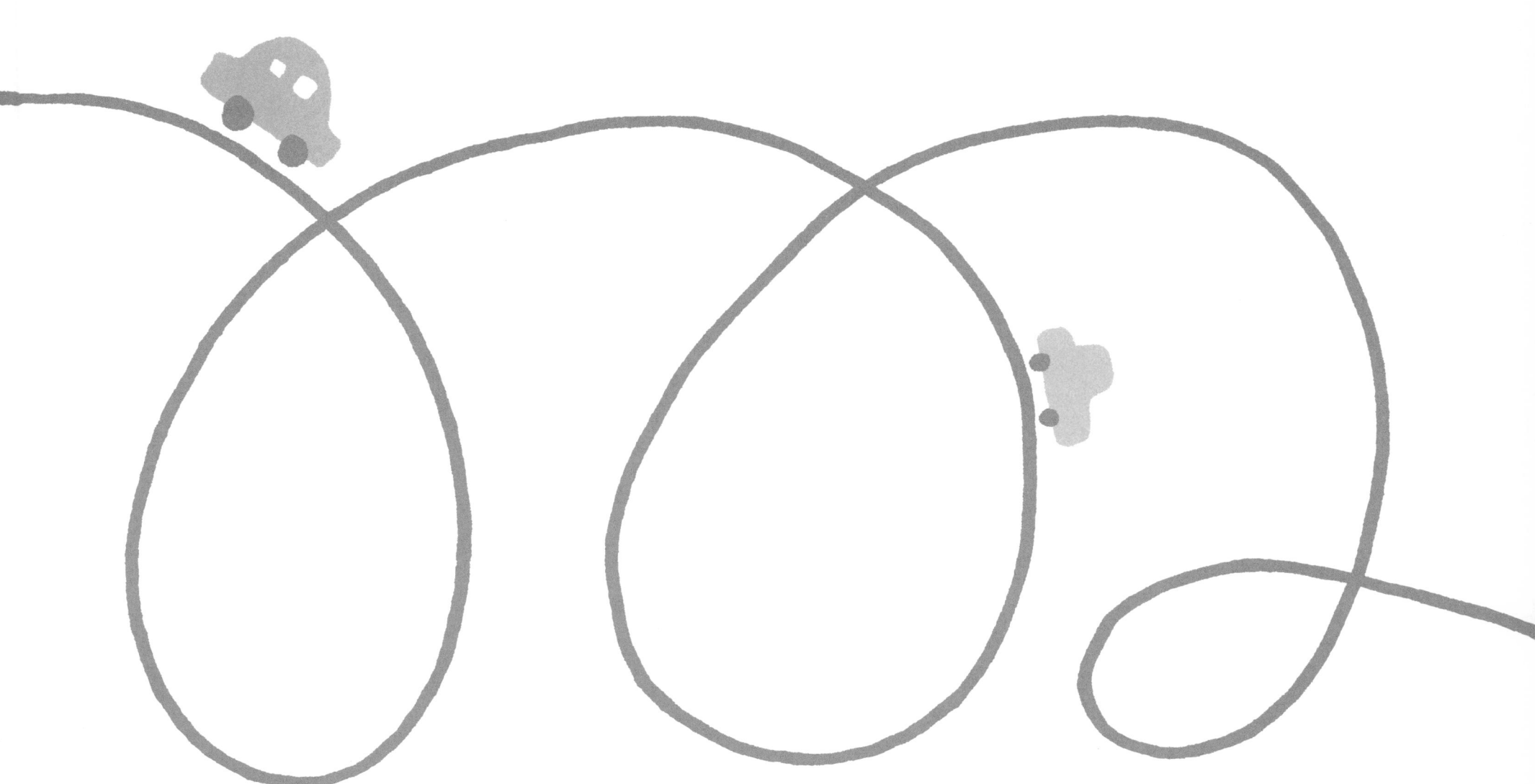

It's a curvy road.

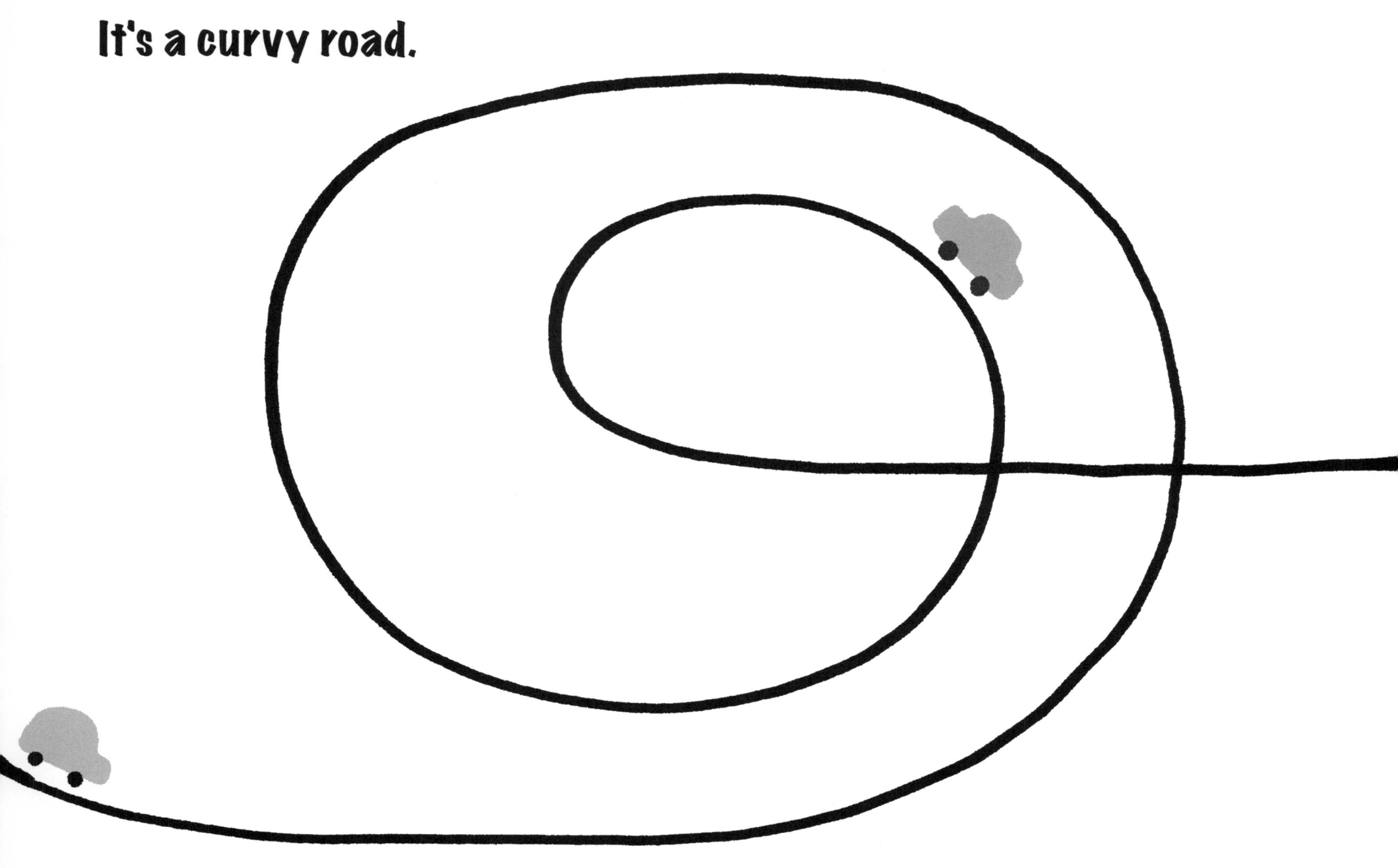

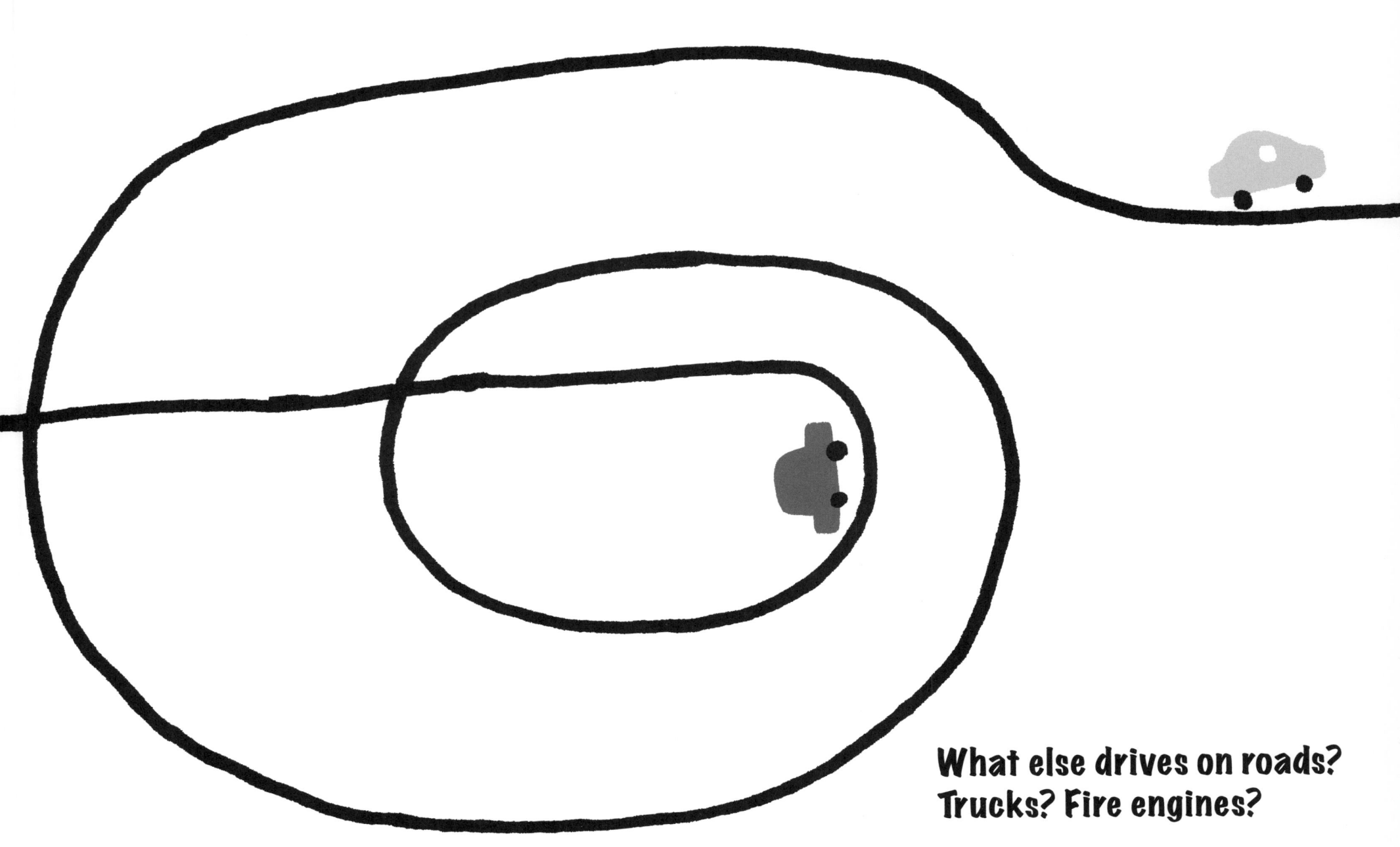

What else drives on roads? Trucks? Fire engines?

These two want to play a trick.

Can you help disguise them?

Decorate the antlers,
and transform the deer!

185

Let's draw masks.

Let's color the houses and draw streets.

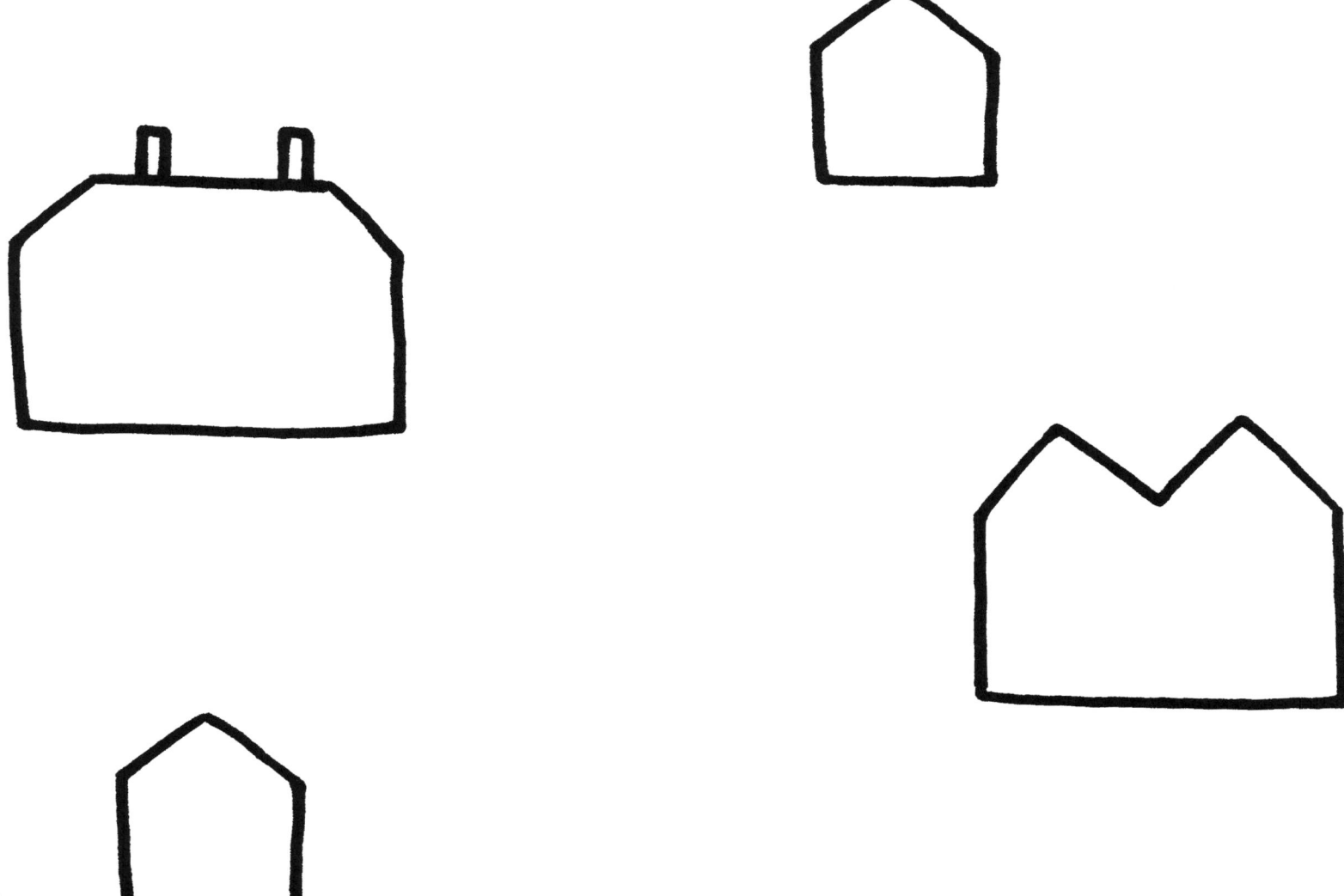

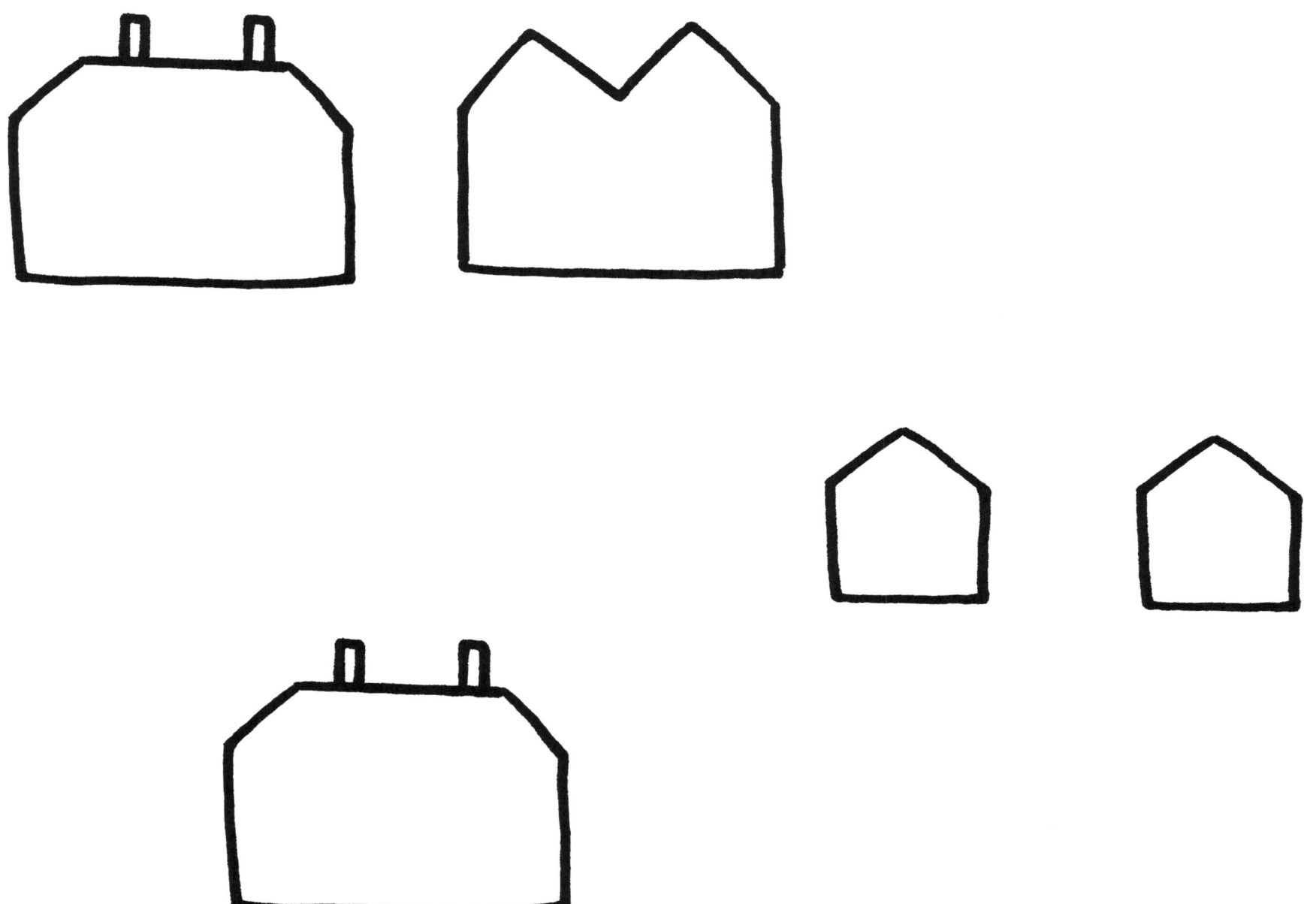

Are these porcupines? Hedgehogs?
Draw what you think!

Ribbons on quills? Sure!

My quills are jagged. Do you think I have enough of them?

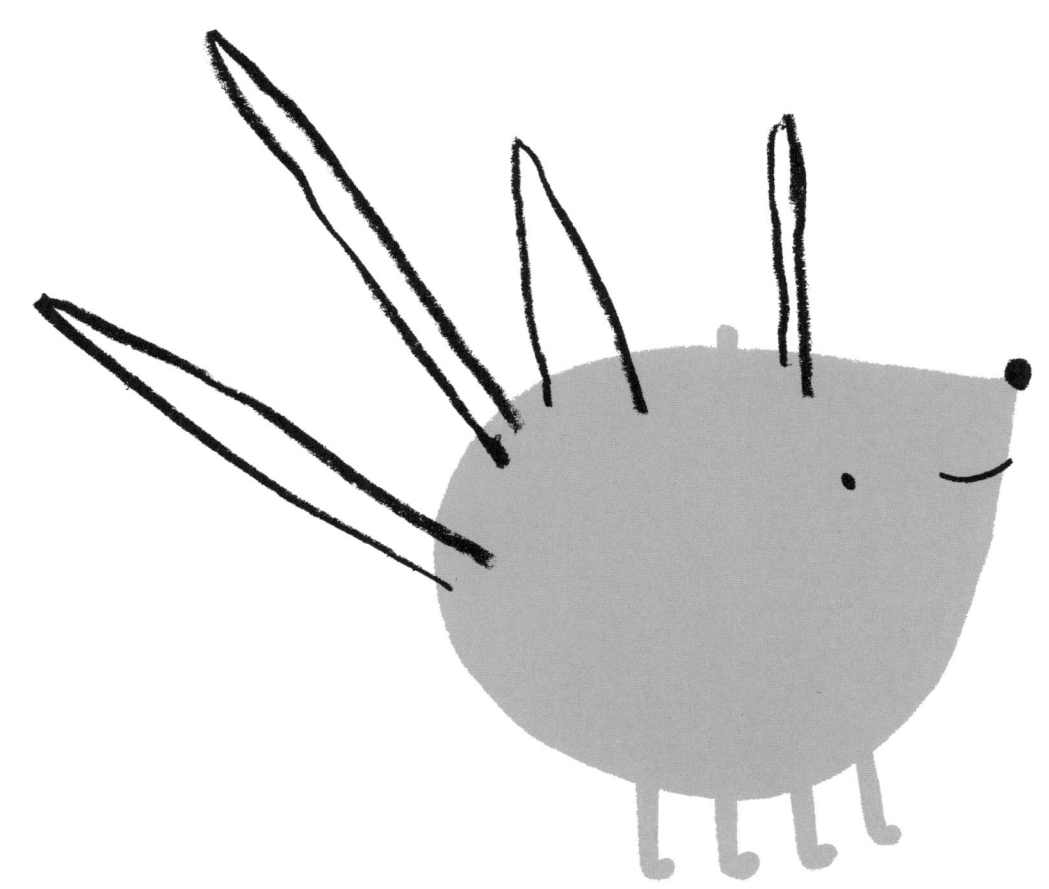

What about me?

There are many types of mustaches.
Put one on everyone.

How do they look?

Is there a story to tell about this whale and the boat?
Draw it in!

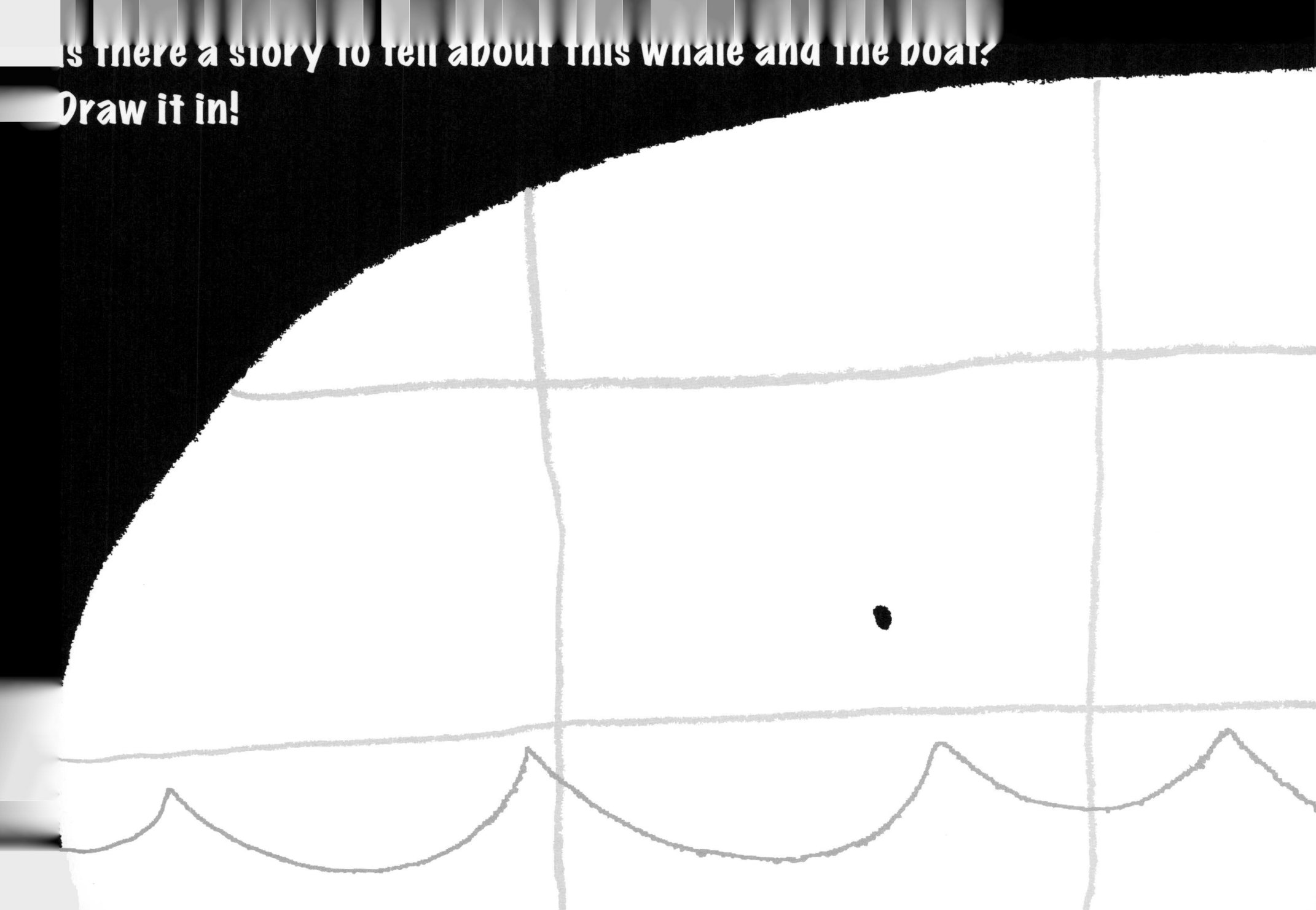

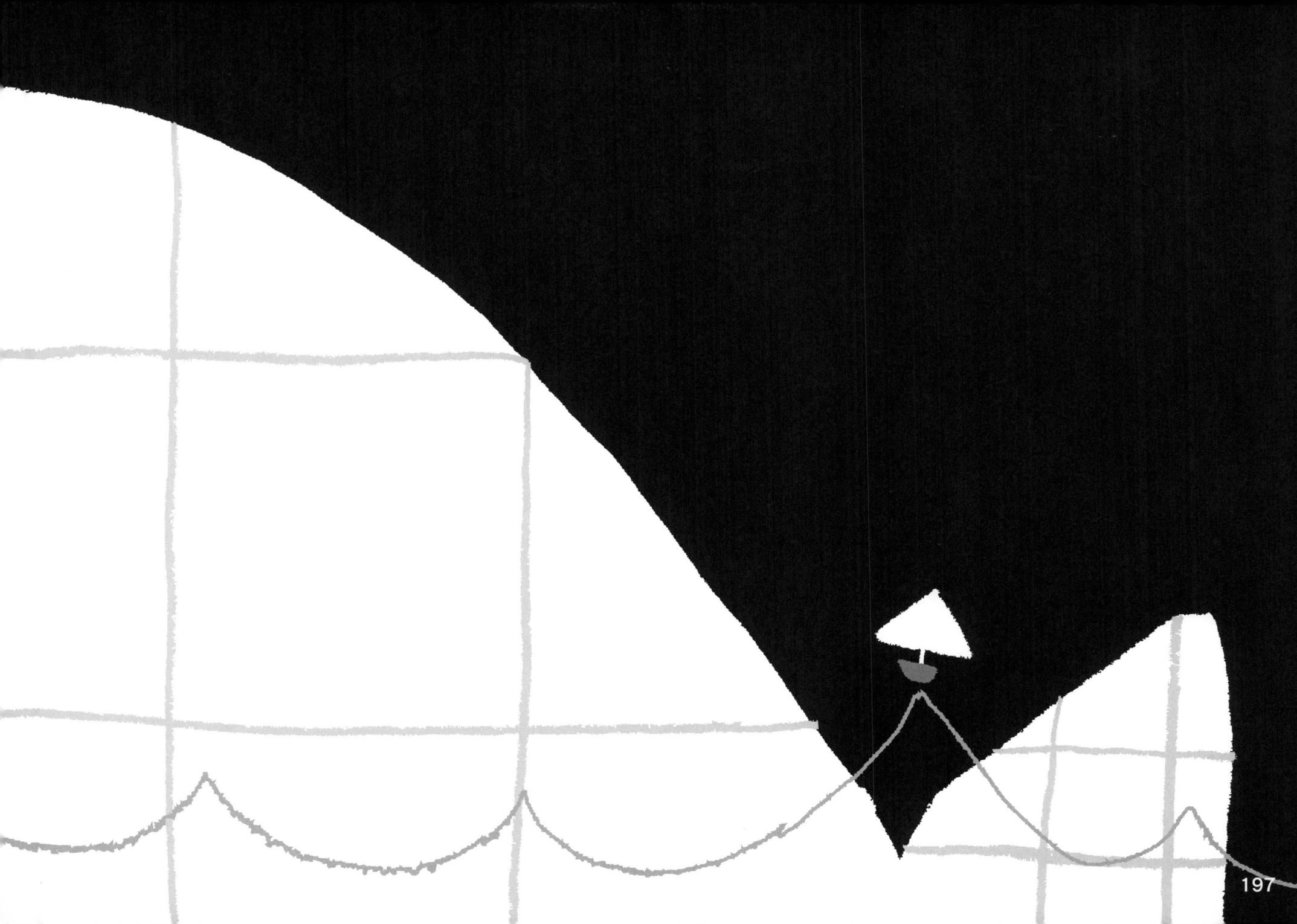

Here is a car. Who is in it? Where is it going?

Also available from Seven Footer Kids:

Asobi no Ousama
Dondon Nuru Hon
©2008 La ZOO / GAKKEN
First published in Japan 2008 by Gakken Co., Ltd.
English translation rights arranged with Gakken Co., Ltd.
through Nextoy, LLC

Published by Seven Footer Kids, an imprint of Seven Footer Press,
a division of Seven Footer Entertainment LLC, NY
Manufactured in Shen Zhen, Guang Dong, P.R.China, in 08/2010 by Printplus Limited.
10 9 8 7 6 5 4 3
© Copyright Seven Footer Kids, 2009 for English Edition
All Rights Reserved
English adaptation designed by Junko Miyakoshi

ISBN 978-1-934734-05-6

www.lazoo.com
www.SevenFooterKids.com

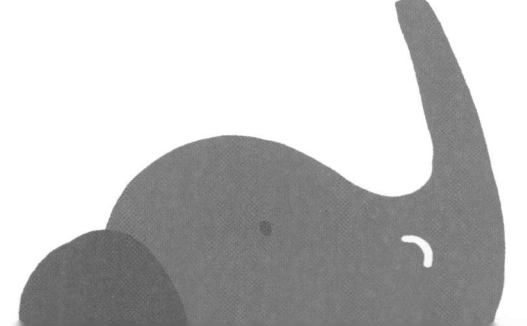